HIZ ♥ HERZ

Greatest Need

&

The Single Biggest Reason Why Marriages Break Down
And How to Build Them Up

Brent Taylor

Published by: Brent W Taylor
brent@hizandherz.ca
Printed in Canada

Scripture quotations are taken from:
Holy Bible, New International Version®, NIV® Copyright ©1973, 1978, 1984, 2011by **Biblica, Inc.®** Used by permission. All rights reserved worldwide.
Also used: Holy Bible, New International Readers Version (NIRV) Copyright ©1995, 1996, 1998, 2014 by **Biblica, Inc.®** Used by permission. All rights reserved worldwide.

Cover design: Brent Taylor
Interior design: Brent Taylor
Author photo: Doreen Vanderhart
Original edition: T. Morgan Editing Services

Taylor, Brent
Hiz and Herz Greatest Need: the single biggest reason marriages break down and how to build them back up / Brent Taylor.

ISBN: 978-0-9959671-0-6 Book
           978-0-9959671-1-3 E-book
           978-0-9959671-2-0 Hardcover book

1. Marriage. 2. Christian Marriage Counseling. 3. Communication in Marriage. 4. Christian Non-Fiction.

For more information about the book, the author, or how to arrange personal marriage and relationship coaching services, speaking events, workshop services, or other services from the author himself, please visit: HizandHerz.ca

Contents

HIZ HERZ

"Happiness is not so much

in having as sharing.

We make a living by what we get,

but we make a life by what we give."

Norman MacEwan

INTRODUCTION

If I could impart a desire in your heart
it would be the gift
to Love
through the hurt.

I wrote this book to give to you the insight I didn't have. Through my pain comes my passion—to share what is not widely known. To help men and women realize their greatest need and the single biggest reason why marriages break down. I've shared the greatest need and the single biggest reason with thousands of men and women who, after hearing it, affirmed it, yet hadn't before realized it.

I hope you will see what to *stop* doing and what you can *start* doing to help build-up your marriage and relationships so you can have more joy, peace and gratitude in your life.

It's not greener on the other side of the fence; it's greener where
you water it.

It took thirty years, three children, two marriages, losing my fifty-million-dollar company, and much heartache before I cracked the mystery—or better yet, my skull—and discovered *Hiz and Herz Greatest Need* and the single biggest reason why marriages break down. The damage I caused to my wife, my children, and my career was more than I could've ever imagined. I felt like I chucked my family over a cliff. Like I threw them away. They were so innocent and never asked for the cruel abandonment.

But, I was still so focused only on what I wanted. I wanted *to be loved*. I wanted what I felt I never had. I didn't realize the destructive impact my choices would have in the lives of my children, my former wife, and other family members. Emotional scars never really go away; they impact the journey of our lives—and can shape our hearts for good. Why didn't I see it sooner? Why don't we see ourselves more clearly? Why are we so selfish and bent on wanting things our own way?

I wondered how long the pain would go on. Then a full-speed-ahead second marriage was even more emotionally damaging. Now the tables were turned. I was reaping what I sowed. You'd think I'd have learned. And as time went on, again my choices hurt the one I love. Causing her to stumble.

Our world is filled with so many broken men and women who keep hurting each other and running away to the next relationship. Looking for love in the circle of fear, not caring about anyone but ourselves—wanting *to be loved*.

When two very broken and selfish people come together, it can be a rough road. It's even more so when the emotional damage from multiple past relationships are brought in. The filters and fears of the past taint our view of the next person, and the next, and the next. We create what we fear, and in turn wind up hurting ourselves and others. I've deeply hurt others and I've been deeply hurt. Selfishness, insecurity, and lack of integrity have been at the root of those hurts. Looking back, I see how choices, upbringing, and thinking patterns played in to how I've lived my life. I have to work at it every day to make healthy changes—working through my fears and practicing loving thoughts. But it is possible to heal and it is possible to return to love. *Love is not selfish.*

When I see a couple hurting, separated, or escaping to another relationship, my heart aches. I want to reach out and let them know it can work if they truly want it to. Many of us deny, distort, and dismiss what we're going through so we don't have to look at ourselves and do the work in our relationship and our thinking. What I've seen is that most men and women don't appreciate how important their spouse is—and how important their marriage is to the lives of others, as well as their own. *Hurt people hurt people.*

So why are we so deceived? Why are we prone to be misguided by friends, family, and society—and yes, even ourselves? Why do so many couples quit instead of commit? Success doesn't happen without giving it our all. So why, then, would we think the most important relationship between two people would be any different? *We can only fix what we acknowledge.*

Is your spouse important enough to set aside your wants so they know you love them? Would a loving parent put their child's needs ahead of their own? We need to look at our attitude—if I leave it up to my spouse, then when is it ever going to work? If it's going to work, it needs to start with me. My attitude is like the aroma of my heart—and *how I treat someone is based on how I see that person.* If I see the negative, then I will manifest the negative, and thus break down the relationship. I need to see the good and work for the good. My spouse needs to know they are worth it.

Ask yourself: How do I see my spouse? How do I treat my spouse? How would my spouse like to be treated?

_____

_____

If I could share with you what makes a man and woman tick, what breaks down their relationship and what builds it up, would you be interested? If you knew you had what it takes to have the marriage you both want—would you do what it takes, with all your heart, all your mind, and all your soul?   Yes_   No_

Love is   more than a feeling
Love is   a choice
Love is   believing

Love is more about the person doing the love than the person who's receiving the love.

Before I could sign the divorce papers, I had to take a course called *Parenting After Separation*. In it, they showed a video of many children from divorced and separated families. The tears, the hurt, and the attempted suicides were heart wrenching to watch. All the children had the same wish. First was that their parents would get back together, and second was that they would quit fighting. I think husbands and wives should take this course before marriage, before having children, and several times after, as a reminder of the hurt children go through when their parents separate and divorce. Many of us haven't been taught how important a loving marriage is for our children.

Mother Teresa was asked: "What can you do to promote world peace?" She answered, "Go home and love your family."

If you want to bust up the world, bust up the family.
If you want to bust up the family, bust up the marriage.

If we look for a *way out* instead of a *way through*, our love for our spouse won't grow. As you read this book, I hope you will see how to save your marriage, enrich your marriage, and realize the back door or over the fence for greener pastures is never the answer. It's true, it takes two to make a marriage, but it's also true that love is contagious. From my heart to yours, you've been given the capacity to love with whatever it takes. The rewards are worth it and everlasting. God bless you.

The roses grow better through the manure, together.

CHAPTER ONE

WE BECOME WHAT WE THINK ABOUT

I am your constant companion.

I am your greatest asset or heaviest burden.

I will push you up to success or down to disappointment.

I am at your command.

Half the things you do might just as well be turned over to me.

For I can do them quickly, correctly, and profitably.

I am easily managed; just be firm with me.

Those who are great, I have made great.

Those who are failures, I have made failures.

I am not a machine, though I work with the precision of a

machine and the intelligence of a person.

You can run me for profit, or you can run me for ruin.

Show me how you want it done. Educate me. Train me.

Lead me. Reward me.

And I will then...do it automatically.

I am your servant.

Who am I?

I am a habit.

Mac Anderson & John J. Murphy

We are creatures of habit. How we were raised as children and how we raise our children significantly impacts how our children think, behave, and what they believe. As we grow, becoming aware of our thought-life and being accountable for our choices is very important. Our cognitive mind loads our non-cognitive mind (i.e., the conscious loads the subconscious). Roughly 90 percent of what we think on and how we behave is based on subconscious patterns.

Believing is a powerful gift we have been given. We're an amazing design. Throughout history we have studied and marvelled at the human brain: the power, the depth of caring, the problem-solving ability, the reasoning, the will, the sensing, the intuitiveness, the beauty, and the mystery.

Yet everything we think about and act on is still a choice: be it happiness, fear, resentment, forgiveness, patience, trusting, distrusting, commitment, hate, or love. So what makes us choose thoughts and behaviours?

The following example below shows how our behaviours and thinking are largely the result of our habits. Example:

Cross your arms in front of your chest. How does that feel? Look at your arms. Now reverse your arms. Most would say this doesn't feel normal. However, if we practice it many times a day for the next few months, it will begin to feel more normal.

Even though new thinking, emotions, and behaviour may not come easily, we can retrain our brain over time and new thinking can become second nature. For those whose spouse likes receiving hugs, I encourage you to start giving hugs several times a day. You'll likely be pleasantly surprised by the positive results.

During my many years of coaching hockey, I would catch some of my players, during practice, cheating on their drills. They wanted to win the little races, but they didn't want to do the hard work. If they cheated, I'd have them do the drills over and over again until they did it right. I'd say to them, "What starts out easy becomes hard and what starts out hard becomes easy."

Words are easy…living them out takes hard work—heart work. But it is only by committing to doing the hard work of changing ourselves for the better that we can reap the benefits of that change.

For much of my life, I've been a talker, a procrastinator, and looking for the pleasures of escape. I became what I practiced. It seems many of us want the icing without baking the cake—we want the romance, sex, fun, and lifestyle without the hard work of commitment. What I've learned from my own experiences is that the sliver of pleasure we find through instant gratification inevitably turns into the mountain of pain. By failing to take our relationships and commitments seriously, we may find a fleeting pleasure, but this pleasure always comes at the expense of the long-lasting, intimate, fulfilling relationship we truly desire in our hearts. I've traded *the sliver of pleasure for the mountain of pain* too many times.

Divorce rates are high, and the number of uncommitted relationships has increased significantly compared to my parents' generation and their parents' generation.

I know in Calgary and Alberta I have seen a huge increase in divorces in the ages between 40 and 60. It seems the boom times bring more greed and selfishness.

Approximately:

40–50%	of 1st time marriages end in divorce
65–80%	of 2nd time marriages end in divorce
80 % plus	of 3rd time marriages end in divorce

Based on various articles, there is a general theme to second and third marriages ending in higher rates. There are various reasons and opinions stated by researchers and authors. However, it's true, we become what we practice and believe. Generally, divorce is rooted in selfishness; divorce is about division not unity. Marriage is about uniting and not self-seeking—it's putting your partner first: PPF. In response to these numbers, some say to me, shouldn't we get better each try? I say, At what? Quitting and starting?

If everyone else is doing it, it's okay…right? I see many young couples that are together but not married. I sense that many have the thinking that if they get married it will end in divorce. Marriage doesn't cause divorce, quitting causes divorce. Whether we realize it or not, we're always modeling character to one another. What we think and do affects others. Instead of quitting and starting, how about committing and finishing?

How many of us have people that will speak into our lives and help build up our marriage instead of just telling us what we want to hear?

Family and friends only hear one side (our side) and they don't want to see us get hurt. So they tend to pull the relationship apart. When we complain about our spouse, friends and family tend to listen and commiserate and support our side of our story in most cases, rather than coming to our spouse's defence or cautioning us to be more sensitive and accepting.

What I've learned about myself is that I had a tendency to dig in my shovel of pride and see my spouse as the problem. When we're hurt, we want to fight or flight, and forgiveness and kindness seem to go out the window.

I hope you'll take ownership of your thinking and behaviours and be cautious when others tell you what you want to hear instead of what you need to hear (e.g., it wasn't meant to be, quit and start over with someone else, move on) instead of what you need to hear (e.g., you need to learn how to love your spouse in the way they need, communicate, stay committed, and work through the hardships, encourage, and forgive).

I say, *keep on, not move on*. A few years ago, my son told me about a poster on his grade-four classroom wall that said, *Don't make excuses—make improvements*.

Right feelings come from doing the right thing. Doing the right thing is rarely achieved when based on feelings. Instead, we typically want it *easy, now, don't pay, and more*. These are dangerous desires for instant gratification.

Wanting it easy means being lazy. Wanting it *now* means we're impatient and usually demanding. Not wanting to pay means we want something for nothing—a sense of entitlement belonging to takers and users not lovers and givers. Chasing the race of *more* usually means being greedy and not content or thankful—never having enough. What we want needs some careful thinking and reflection of our heart. We need to always strive to identify our *motive*. Many of us don't like to change, or see the need to change, our thinking. Yet, there is one thing that brings about change: pain. When the pain is greater than the fear of change, that's when we change. In the book *Dare to Dream* by Curt Marsh, an NFL all-star football player who lost his leg, he says, "We've been given the capacity to handle whatever comes our way." I like how he put it: "given" and "whatever comes our way." I believe we've been given this gift. Our biggest difficulties give us the opportunity for character growth.

Marriage takes a lot of work. That's why it is the most beautiful relationship between man and woman. Husband and Wife are a team for life, no matter what feelings come and go. *Our word* needs to be more important than *our want*.

Love always perseveres. Marriage is about couples who are committers, not quitters. The book by Dr. Caroline Leaf, *Switch On Your Brain,* lets us know we can retrain our brain to create new thinking and emotional patterns. She quotes from the Bible, "For God has not given us a spirit of fear, but of power and of love and of a sound mind." (2nd Timothy 1:7).

We become what we practice, whether it's intentional, instinctive, or how we were raised and treated from infancy into our early adult years. Our thinking is linked to emotion. We build memories through our experiences and our memories store emotions. There is always some type of emotion tied to our thinking. Every decision we make is impacted by emotion. Babies, young children, and young adults gain most of their thinking and emotional patterns from their parents and others that are close to them. The brain absorbs massive quantities of information from the environment and develops significantly during the first few years after being born.

Most of what you think and do is habitual. Roughly 90% or more of the action in your mind is in your subconscious (non-conscious). The subconscious drives the conscious. The conscious mind, where up to 10% of the mind action occurs, is much slower and is more controlled. The conscious (cognitive) mind in turn drives the output of what you say and do (the output of your thinking). As well, information comes in through the five senses (sight, sound, smell, taste, touch) and is received by the conscious (cognitive) mind. The conscious mind is where your creative and consequential thinking occurs (your wishes, desires, aspirations). Therefore, it is important to be careful and deliberate about our thinking, emotions, and choices.

We have been given choice. Good feelings will come from good choices. This requires insight and discipline to retrain our brain from earlier years. If we want to change our toxic or unloving thoughts and emotions, we will need to learn how to do this and what to focus on. Teaching ourselves and our children to focus on responsible and loving thoughts is important to our relationships and our wellbeing. *As the saying goes, of course, old habits die hard.*

My mom once said to me, "I'm sure your dad would like to change things about me, but he really has never said much." And then she said, "There're things that I'd like to change about him." And then, in a bit of a sad tone, she concluded, "We really are fault finders." I wish I'd kept this in the front of my mind more—if I had, I may have not tried to change the one I love, or have been so controlling and ungrateful. Please see the good in the one you love—I believe you will be thankful and have more peace in your life if you do.

My parents are in their seventies now and they've had some real tough times, yet they are still together and their relationship is growing richer as I write these words. I am grateful they are my parents. Growing old together is something worth aspiring toward in marriage. Running amok in youth may entertain us at the time, but as we grow older, none of us want to grow lonelier. We all want someone beside us to support us as we travel through the ups and downs of life—especially the downs. But if we want such a long-lasting and true love, we must be equally willing to stand beside our spouse during all of their highs and all of their lows. We must be willing to sacrifice and work hard for the one we love, and to commit ourselves completely—body, mind, and soul.

When we recognize our own thoughts and behaviours, and how they either support or undermine our relationships, plus make the needed changes, we are doing the hard work necessary to make our love last. If you truly love your spouse and want to grow old with them, to raise a loving family, and to have children who love and admire you both when you're old and gray, this is the work you must commit to.

CHAPTER TWO

WHAT'S MY MOTIVE?

When you want the best for someone, how do you treat them? Take time to think on this and be honest. Ask yourself, "Do I criticize and control or preach and pressure? Or, do I truly want the best for the one I love? And if so, what do I think would be the best for the one I love?" Next, what do you think your spouse (or loved one) would say is best for them? Then ask, "How would I know if I'm on the right track?" Stop and write down these questions—then answer them as best as you can.

As you read, you may glean more insight to these questions. I encourage you to take some time to write down your thoughts and answers. What we do, think, say, or feel is an expression of love or a calling for love. Do you think about your motive before you speak, act, and decide? Do you know when your motive is of love or selfishness?

Love is patient. Love is kind. It does not want what belongs to others. It does not brag. It is not proud. It does not dishonor other people. It does not look out for its own interests. It does not easily become angry. It does not keep track of other people's wrongs. Love is not happy with evil. But it is full of joy when the truth is spoken. It always protects. It always trusts. It always hopes. It never gives up.

Love never fails. But prophecy will pass away. Speaking in languages that had not been known before will end. And knowledge will pass away.

1st Corinthians 13: 4-8

This wedding vow is a life-long marriage vow for the most significant relationship that exists between two human beings. It's completeness and truth has been shared in the hearts of men and women across the world. I'm told it's the number one definition of love as recognized by psychologists.

Ask yourself, "Am I expressing love (giving), or am I calling for love (getting)?" Be careful, not to give to get.

The opposite of Love is self-seeking and control.

So what are some ways to build your relationship?

When you feel like you're being controlled or controlling, what can you do? How about: Let Go and Love.

I would suggest many of us are calling for love versus expressing love much of the time. Ask your spouse: What can I do for you today? How can I love you today?

A woman longs for her husband to be thoughtful. Love requires thoughtfulness from both, which is about building bridges. Love teaches you how to meet in the middle, to respect and appreciate how each other thinks and feels.

Motive. In our world, many are focused on status, popularity, appearance, and wealth. We're absorbed in ourselves more than we care about others. I was having dinner with my son when he was going through some real rough times. I told him that we tend to live in one of three places: I'm not good enough, I'm not as bad the other guy, and I'm better than the other guy. I said, "These are the wrong places to live."

He said, "I've been living there a lot." Why are so many of us worried about what others think of us? Yet, when I reach out in kindness to others, it's way better.

Not everyone may appear to be overly focused on appearance, status, or what others think. Yet, most of us are fairly self-centered. If my forehead were a television screen, there would be a lot of movies about me.

The size of my diamond ring, my wardrobe, my house, my truck, my company, my boobs or my biceps...these things shouldn't define me.

Notice Me, Get Me, Love Me, Understand Me, Respect Me

What defines *me*—my standard of living or my standard of giving?

There are only two Motives

LOVE	SELFISHNESS
Patient, Kind,	Controlling, Greedy,
Respect, Humble,	Rude, Boastful, Pride
Honesty, Trusting,	Lying, Cheating,
Commitment, Perseverance	Denial, Quitting,
Compassion, Listening	Fear, Hiding, Escaping,
Honouring, Serving, Faithful,	Pity Me Worry, Gossip
Forgiving, Protects,	Blame, Resentment
Willing to Sacrifice.	Self – Seeking.

Relationships can be our greatest source of pleasure or our greatest source of pain. Do you recall a time when you were hurt or betrayed? Or when you were the betrayer or rejecter? Remember, *the heart of the problem is the problem of the heart.* In Dr. Caroline Leaf's book *Switch On Your Brain* she states there are roughly 700 to a 1000 trillion cells in the body. All of these cells have been found to respond not only to external stimuli as we would expect, but also

26

to our *emotions*. When we feel bad, feelings like resentment and anger are actually causing damage to our bodies—we're making ourselves sick. But when we release those bad feelings and allow feelings of love and acceptance to fill our beings, our bodies actually begin to heal themselves! One of the most powerful healing emotions is forgiveness.

When there is forgiveness there is healing at the cellular level. Selfishness holds on to anger and resentment and sorrow. *Love* forgives.

Looking at the two motives—Love versus Selfishness—ask yourself which motive has been more prominent in your life? In what situations or contexts does each motive tend to present itself? Understanding our thoughts and behaviors means understanding the motives that are behind them. In any situation, we must stop and examine our thoughts and behaviors and ask ourselves: *Why am I thinking this? Why am I behaving this way? Is it love that is guiding my actions, or am I acting out of selfish desire to get what I want?* When you argue with your spouse, is it loving? Or is it an attempt to get your own way?

When you are gentle and kind to your spouse, is it love, or is it manipulation? Are you giving for the sake of giving, or are you giving in order to get something out of it?

When our motive is love, we give love, build love, and are then open to receiving love. When our motive is selfishness, we cannot give love, we cannot build love, and we deny ourselves the possibility of receiving love. It is only when acting out of love that we can receive love in return.

CHAPTER THREE

THE CANDY STORE & BAKING THE CAKE

If you put a boy in a candy store and take the lids off all the candy jars, and the storekeeper walks out, what's likely to happen? He'll probably take the candy. I say, "Girls, don't take your lids off."

A wise lady once told me that w*omen give sex to get love and men give love to get sex.* Unfortunately, this assumes that sex is not part of love. Sex is an amazing part of love and marriage. We know that oxytocin and other endorphins are released and bring about that euphoric sense of connection, oneness, and commitment between man and woman.

I've let selfish desire take over many times in my life, but what I really wanted was to share my life with the one I love. Investing in someone and saving ourselves for the one we want and waiting for the right time seems so void in our thinking and values today. Relationships have become disposable. Why do we throw them out and move on to the next sensation, the next relationship? It's a shallow and empty way to live.

Shannon Ethridge and Stephen Arterburn write, in *Every Woman's Battle: Discovering God's Plan for Sexual and Emotional Fulfilment,* that women have been using their bodies to get what they want since biblical times. In my view, many men have done the dishonourable act of stealing the candy and pursuing the innocent with selfish motives. Desires can be delightful, but they can also be dangerous. Life is full of fine lines that test our character.

We need to be careful and watch out for those wow-now desires! It's easy to rationalize, justify, and escape out the back door with an attitude that a better offer might come along. We seem to be creating a new norm in our society where we think this behaviour is acceptable, but selfish temptation can be deceiving and have damaging results.

Bake the cake, then add the icing. If you just go for the icing, the cake doesn't get baked.

Sexual & Physical Intimacy and Connection

The spark that ignites the chemical reaction and fire between man and woman. Yet it is really deepened when the relational foundation is strong.

The Cake, AKA Foundation, which will weather the storms and be committed to doing what it takes.

Friendship, Trust, Forgiveness, Honesty, Willingness to Understand and Listen, Emotional Vulnerability, Patience, For Each Other Through Thick and Thin, Fewer Expectations, Acceptance, Honour, Flexibility, Common Values/Interests/Beliefs.

Girls: if you want to damage the quality of your relationship for the future, just give the candy (yourself) away early.

Let me tell you a secret. Here is what a lot of guys think: "If she gives me the candy too soon," in the back of his mind, he thinks, "she's sleazy-easy." He struggles with respecting her (and himself, yet won't admit his own wrong).

And if he can't respect her, he'll struggle with trusting her. Later he can become jealous, which damages the relationship further. Guys think, "If she'll be sleazy-easy with me, she will do it with another guy."

This may not be the case from the girl's perspective, but often it is from his. When the relationship struggles with the lack of trust, the friendship and love are significantly strained. So if you want to increase the chances of having a healthy relationship, then take time to build friendship, trust, respect, and love—to honour one another. Marriage is about commitment, and having casual sex outside of marriage is not being committed to each other. Remember, the sliver of pleasure usually turns out to be the mountain of pain—one or both of you are bound to end up hurt. Also remember your motive for giving away, or taking, the candy. Giving to get is not giving—it's manipulating.

Girls: if you want to trust him, then you need to show him you are trustworthy.

Guys: it's up to the man to show honour and be the man. Falling to temptation is not a sign of strength, integrity, or respect. *Love is about honour, not on-her.* If you can't respect her in the early stages of your relationship, what's the chance of the relationship being built on a foundation of respect that weathers the storms in the future?

Chasing the romance and physical love (*eros* love— the icing) is dangerous. If it causes you to keep getting in and out of relationships, and it starts to become an emotional pattern of striving for the next and newest sensation, then check your motive. Sex is not much different than other addictions or escapes. When you love them and leave them it not only hurts them, but also causes major damage to *your* ability to have a committed relationship that builds a deeper love over time.

Unfortunately, this is often not understood by those who keep getting in and out of relationships. Like a sticky-note when first stuck on a paper or a wall, the more you stick it on and off, the less it sticks. Well, the same happens to your ability to love. The words "I love you" don't mean much when thrown around so freely. This is not to say that we should withhold these words for only the most special of occasions—to do so can actually damage relationships between spouses as well as between parents and children by making them question if they are loved. It leads to life-long insecurities. We should tell those we love that we love them as *much* as possible!

But we *should* withhold these words for people closest to our heart. By telling someone that we love them in an effort to manipulate them into giving us what we want, we are diminishing the value of our words and disrespecting them as well as the very meaning of love. It's only when we truly love someone that we should tell them so. When we express our love purely and without ulterior motives, we are *giving* love and therefore opening ourselves to receive love in return.

As we've discussed, we become what we practice—including our habits, insecurities, and fears. Do not make a habit out of expressing your *"love"* in a selfish effort to control, manipulate, or otherwise get what you want in a situation. An expression of love, whether through words or through physical intimacy, should only occur when your motive is to give love without expectation of reward. But how do we know that it is true love that we feel? In the beginning of a relationship, we can't trust our feelings right away. We may think that we feel an instant and powerful love upon meeting someone, but often this feeling is actually lust or infatuation. It is only by taking the time to get to know each other, building trust and respect, and nurturing a firm foundation of friendship, that we can know that what we felt for a person is love. Respect yourself and respect your mate by taking this time and committing yourselves to each other—baking the cake—before you allow yourselves to indulge in the icing.

Remember, true love—deeper love, unconditional love, *agape* undeserved love—is not just the sensual feelings of eros or sexual love. We all say and do things that hurt others or betray the ones we love, even if it is subtle. We criticize when we should encourage, we blame instead of taking accountability. We hold grudges instead of forgiving.

We all want to be loved unconditionally and to be accepted for who we are—just as we are. We often judge others by their actions and want others to judge us by our intentions.

Agape love is unconditional love, undeserved love, and a love that forgives all wrongs. It's not natural for us to do this. It's extremely difficult. It is divine love, yet a love we all truly want. When we love others with this kind of love, it brings healing and closeness that is tender and humble. It's a deep compassion that looks beyond fears and insecurities. Pride and self-centered ego can get in our way of making amends. But, true love bears all things. It's God's love He gives to us to give to each other. The one who loves is filled up and so is the one being loved. Agape love holds no record of wrongs, it cancels the debt and sacrifices for the benefit of the other. It honours the One who gives us this love each and every day.

CHAPTER FOUR

I'LL NEVER GET A GIRL LIKE THAT AGAIN

When I first met Jimmy, we were at lunch with a common friend. We had a long lunch and talked about quite a bit. I told him what I'm passionate about and we chatted about life in general.

The next time we met for coffee, he showed me a picture of his girlfriend on Facebook. He mentioned that he broke up with her because she was too needy—and that she was very upset with him over something he had done. I asked why she was upset. He explained that he had written something on Facebook. I asked, "What did you write?"

He said, "The truth."

Again I asked, "What did you write?"

He said, "A woman chooses a man to fill her many needs and a man chooses many women to fill his one need."

I asked him, "How do you think that makes her feel? She probably feels like she's just one of many women to fill your one need. That she's not important to you."

He shrugged it off. He said his friends said that if she can't take it she isn't worth it.

The next time we met, he showed me a picture of another girl—she looked a lot like the first girl, go figure.

He said, "We're just friends."

I smiled and asked, "Have you had sex yet?"

He sighed, answering, "Yeah, twice."

I shook my head.

He said, "Come on, you can't tell me women don't want sex the same as men."

I said, "Yes, but for more reasons than you realize."

Most girls want to know that *I'm his* and *he is mine.* They want the security of a relationship and knowing that you are together and she is not just a play toy.

He made a face like he knew what I was saying, yet brushed it off nonetheless. He then told me about another girl. He said, "There's this one girl from Slovakia who was marriage material."

I asked, "Why is she marriage material?"

He said, "Because she's saving herself for marriage." Again I asked, "Why is she marriage material?"

He said, "I can trust her."

We chatted for a while more and then didn't see each other for months.

Then, out of the blue, he called and said, "Brent, you will never guess what happened! You'd be proud of me."

I said, "What happened?"

He said, "There's this girl I met on Facebook. She came to see me. She's the most beautiful, hottest babe I've ever seen." He continued, "You know when you walk into the bar and every guy's head turns—you've got the hottest babe! She's had a boob job and everything. We played mini golf, had a few drinks, and went back to the house. We started making out. I can't believe I was such an idiot. I'll never get a girl like that again."

"What happened?" I asked.

"She took her clothes off." Again, he said, "I'm such an idiot. I told her I can't. She was upset, asking what's wrong are you not attracted to me. I said no, just the opposite, but I'm not comfortable. I told her that I wanted to get to know her first. She started to cry—we just cuddled on the couch for an hour and a half." He repeated, "I'll never get a girl like that again."

I said, "Hold it, Jimmy. You probably showed her more love in an hour and a half than all the guys she's taken her clothes off for in the last several years." I reassured him, "You'll get a girl like that again. And more importantly, you showed her real love. You had courage to honour her."

As I write these words, I look at my own actions and motives in the past…and I should've had the courage to do what Jimmy did. How many of us can see ourselves in this story? How many of us men did not show the woman in our life the honour she deserved (real love)? How many women have reached out for love and given themselves away too soon? How many of us are willing to say sorry and forgive each other and build a relationship of Love and Respect that has deep commitment and honour for each other? Relationships don't always start right, yet with two humble and forgiving hearts, the wrongs of the past can be put right for the future.

Yes, many women like to be pursued, but most don't like a needy man. Wow! This is a fine line and a moving target. Some women play hard to get or push him away to see if he really means it. When she does, it can make him try harder and cause him to appear needy. Many guys do like to pursue but can't read a girl's mind to know if she is pushing him away because she wants him to follow, or if she genuinely does not want to be pursued. I'm sure you have seen the email with all the buttons on the control panel.

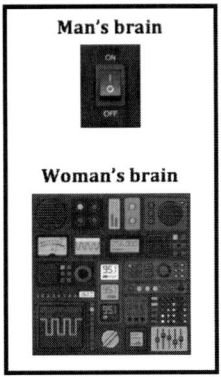

There is a book called *Make Up, Don't Break Up* written by Dr. Bonnie Eaker Weil. It suggests that there is often a pursuer and a distancer in a marriage. Usually, the more the pursuer pursues the more the distancer distances. So if a pursuer backs off it is reasonable that the distancer will feel less pressure and not be so distant, possibly moving towards the pursuer. This is a delicate balance to maintain and one needs to check their motive when doing so, as most of us tend to be self-seeking. To get upset with someone because they are not performing in the way we would like is not fair or mature—*we're not mind readers.* Spouses both must take equal responsibility in communicating with each other so that needs can be met effectively and miscommunication doesn't result in disaster. As Mark Gungor says in his book *Laugh Your Way to a Better Marriage,* many of us think we are going to understand our spouse through osmosis, but there's a better way: *we can ask.*

You might be saying, "Okay, I get men and women are different and marriage takes work, but what's the *greatest need* of men and women in a marriage, and what's the single biggest reason why marriages break down?"

CHAPTER FIVE

HIZ & HERZ GREATEST NEED   &

*The Single Biggest Reason Why Marriages Break Down
And How to Build Them Back Up*

In this chapter, we will discuss what I call our *Greatest Need* in our relationships, as well as what can happen when that need is not being met and, most importantly, what we can do to remedy the effects of that unmet need in our marriage.

Men and women in a relationship each have a single, primary need that drives them. This need is not the same for husband and wife but, rather, tends to differ based on gender. Women's primary need in a relationship is different from men's primary need in that same relationship, but these needs are nonetheless equal and complementary to each other. When one or both spouses suffer from an unmet primary need in their marriage, the marriage inevitably breaks down. Because their primary need is often left unrecognized by their spouse, this breakdown can be difficult to repair without mutual effort and communication. Often, our need is so innate that we, ourselves, may not even understand it or be able to name it, let alone be able to communicate it to our spouse.

In working with men and women, I focus on three primary areas to help them in their relationships. These three areas are: **U**nderstanding, **C**ommunication, and a **G**iving heart (**U C G**), which are further explained in chapters 6, 7, and 8. Now on to the greatest need, breakdown, and how to build it up.

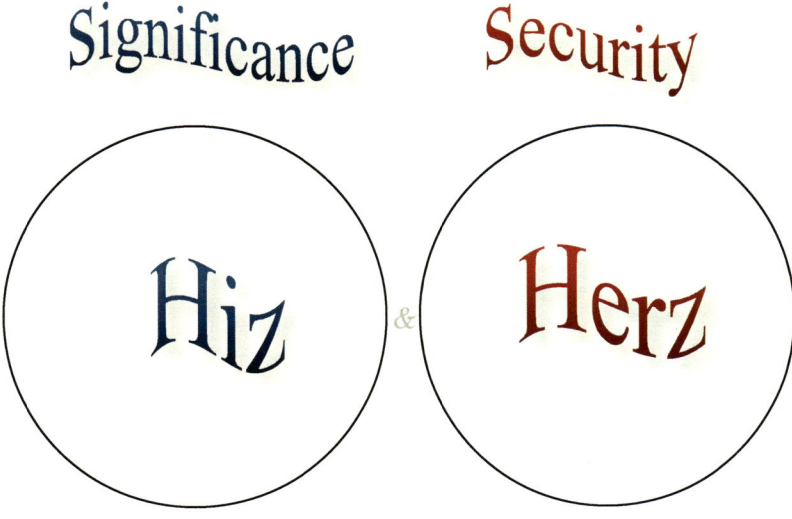

A man's greatest need (in some form) is Significance.

A woman's greatest need is Security (Emotional and Physical)

Certainly, we all have many other needs, but it is men's primary need for a feeling of significance, and women's primary need for a feeling of security, that are most integral to our relationships. These needs give insight into how we want to be loved at our very core.

Let me start off by sharing with you my Coin Theory. On one side of the coin, in the beginning of the relationship, the *Sex* and the *Roses* were great! He felt like number one and she was going to live happily ever after!

But then the white picket fence comes along. She finds herself trying to drag his butt over to the other side of the fence, which needs commitment and responsibility, and he's saying it's not as fun over here.

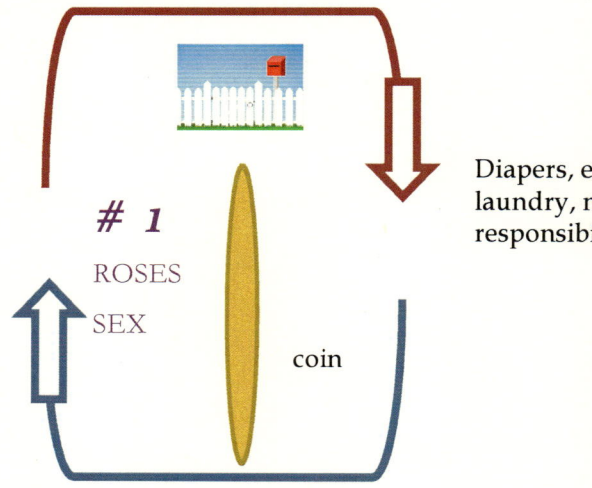

Ladies, he still needs you to play over here where you found him—the things that drew him into the relationship in the beginning are still important to him as the relationship progresses.

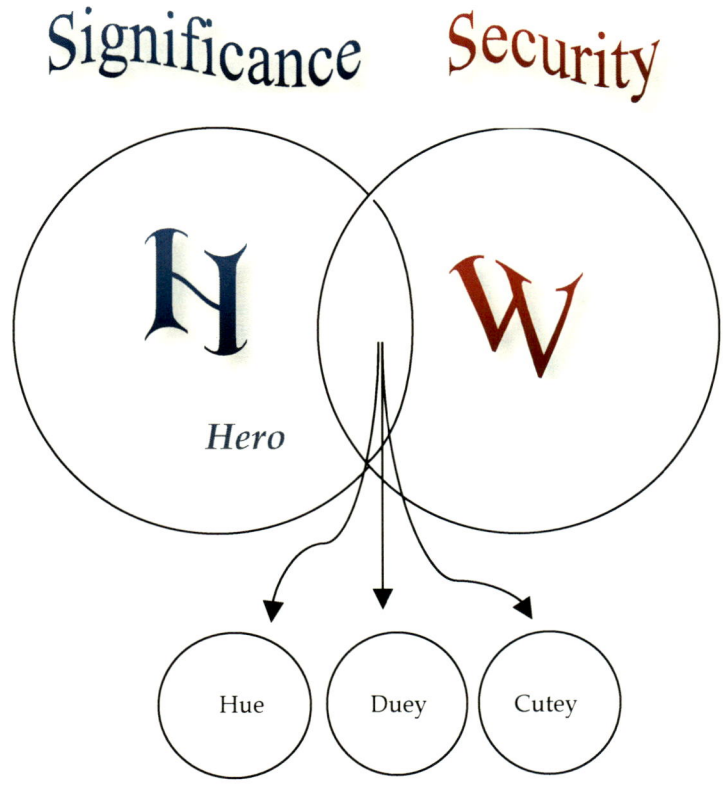

Significance   Security

H   W

Hero

Hue   Duey   Cutey

After the children come along, our married couple finds that something changes...*she's changed.* Her number one priority has suddenly shifted. Her attention naturally becomes focused primarily on the children, often at the expense of her husband. At some point, every guy will feel like he's less important—not number one anymore. She doesn't get why he doesn't get what she is getting. And he usually doesn't know how to handle it or talk about it. He hasn't had the same internal change that she has, nor was he really prepared for this shift in their relationship. Every man wants to be his wife's *hero*. He might suck at it, but he still wants to be her number one.

When a man and woman have sex, the neurotransmitter *oxytocin* is released. This chemical strengthens the bond of love between them—it's the commitment chemical in our brains that makes us want to be together forever. This is an amazing chemical bond that creates a oneness between two people. It fills each other's cup. But now that the children are born, Mom is also getting her cup filled from her interactions with them, not to mention the priority she now places on meeting their children's needs. This is, in part, because oxytocin is also released in huge amounts during childbirth, and when nursing and interacting with her baby. Men experience oxytocin release around their children too, but in far more conservative quantities.

This is not to say that men experience less love for their children, by any means, but rather to emphasize that when the baby is born and during the first few years of life, the mother has a natural physiological reaction to the baby that ensures she will dedicate herself fully to meeting the baby's needs, thus better ensuring its survival and development. There is a special bond Mom has with the children at early ages that dads often don't quite get. Fathers have been shown to contribute more to the childrearing process once the children are older—around toddler and school age. Before this, though they may love and tend to their children, their role is somewhat limited because babies have a greater need for their mothers at this early stage of their life.

With this change in the family dynamics, a man's desire for his wife can seem to go up, all the while Mom's desire and time is taken up with the children. Therefore, in a way, the children are pulling the teeter-totter out of balance from the way it used to be. This can be extremely confusing and disheartening for the husband, as he feels left out and excluded. His sense of his own significance to his wife and family is often abruptly lessened and may not rise back to previous levels for years after the baby is born—this can be compounded when the family continues to grow and Mom is constantly focused on the newest addition to the family.

When a man feels insignificant, his typical reaction is to *retreat*. He goes inside himself and withdraws. This is a *fear*-based emotional response. When not feeling like he is wanted or important to his wife, he often withdraws from his wife and his children. This is far more common for men than it is for women. His logic is that he must not be as important to her as he used to be. Many men can turn to other escapes or coping behaviours (e.g., work, drinking, porn, gambling, television, etc.)—when deep inside, what he really wants is his wife. He wants to feel like he matters to her again. He wants to feel significant. When a man retreats, her need for *security* is threatened and she can be left feeling extremely *insecure*. She's often just as confused by the change in their relationship as he is, but from her perspective life is wonderful and fulfilling and they have a beautiful baby together, yet for some reason he is pulling away from their family. She has feelings of abandonment and can't understand what his problem is.

This, too, is a *fear*-based emotional response. It's a natural reaction. Even if he hasn't left physically, he may be emotionally withdrawn. It feels to her like he doesn't want what she wants and is abandoning her and the children. Her typical reaction is to *attack* or *reject* her husband—a basic fight or flight instinct when faced with a threatening situation. When she is attacking, she's trying to say "Don't you abandon me!" When she's rejecting, she's trying to protect herself from his rejection by rejecting him first, saying, "I don't need you anyway!" Because, if she doesn't need him, his rejection can't hurt her—or so she convinces herself to keep her heart safe. She doesn't even realize she is doing it. This is a typical, natural response made out of fear and the need for security. Women can also turn to escapes as well in this situation (e.g., friends, other men, etc.).

Though this situation is bad enough as it is, because the husband and wife are not communicating, rather, reacting on instinct and lashing out at each other, it tends to spiral and get even *worse*. When she attacks or rejects him, he feels even *more* insignificant to her—the one person he wants to be most significant to is rejecting or attacking him—so he retreats some more, making her feel even more insecure, and her insecurity causes her to attack or reject again.

And around and around it goes, with the gap getting wider and wider. More fear, more blame, and more hurt—building and building until both don't even know why it all started or how to get out of the mess. This is just one of the marital circumstances in which this cycle can occur. I use it here because it's the most prominent. This same cycle can occur as a result of any marital issues that arise. Financial problems are also a commonly cited reason for divorce—but finances aren't the real reason behind a couple getting divorced.

The reason behind a broken relationship is almost always that one spouse's greatest need was not being met and, as a result of this unmet need, the couple spiraled into this cycle. The finances may cause the wife to feel insecure, so she lashes out and attacks or rejects her husband—her way of begging for that security to be restored—who then feels like his wife doesn't value him anymore and so he withdraws from her. The cycle repeats until it culminates in total marital breakdown. Self-awareness, a willingness to change, and a skilled and knowledgeable marriage counsellor can help prevent and repair such tragic misunderstandings. Keep in mind it will depend on you and your spouse doing the hard work – the heart work – over the long haul to bring about the loving changes you need. We get more of what we don't want by trying to get what *we* want instead of finding out what it is our *spouse* wants and needs from us. It's unawareness and fear that keep the relationship in turmoil until someone says, *I'm done* or, hopefully, *Let's get some help*.

Marriages break up for emotional reasons and these reasons are difficult to talk about for fear of making it worse or being vulnerable. Sometimes we don't even recognize the reasons ourselves in order to be able to communicate them to our spouse, which is why enlisting outside help can make such a difference in the outcome of marital disputes.

Until we understand this and see the pattern, we won't begin to take the needed steps to change. Unfortunately, most couples have been modeled this behaviour by their own parents and others in their lives, and not taught how to love their mates in the way that they need to be loved. I have affirmed this by surveying over 5,000 men and women, as well as researching books and attending conferences, and all avenues of inquiry I've examined have led me straight back to this conclusion.

Now that you are aware of your own greatest need and that of your spouse, and can see how it affects your behaviors in times of stress, I hope you can take this insight and use it to help you break the cycle that ends marriages.

Not only can you use this knowledge to save your marriage, you can also use it to *enrich* your marriage by ensuring that you pay close attention to your spouse's need for Significance or Security so that you can take positive, affirming steps toward keeping it fulfilled.

Caring for your spouse's greatest need benefits the entire family. When the parents are happy, the children are happy too.

When a man loves his children, picks up the vacuum, make arrangements for date night or family time, and makes dinner, *he is loving his wife*. He is fulfilling *her* need for a sense of *security* by demonstrating how important his family is to him and making concrete efforts to love his family and keep them healthy and safe.

When a wife is loving her husband, *she is loving her children* (e.g., Believing in him, cheer-leading him, and respecting him, not mothering him, and making requests not demands, etc.). She is fulfilling his need to feel significant, and in doing so shows him how important he is to her and their family, which encourages him to stay engaged and benefits the kids by giving them an active, loving, and supportive father.

Moms often default to loving their children first. Caution is needed towards the balance in the family. How is her husband and how much control are the children having in the family.

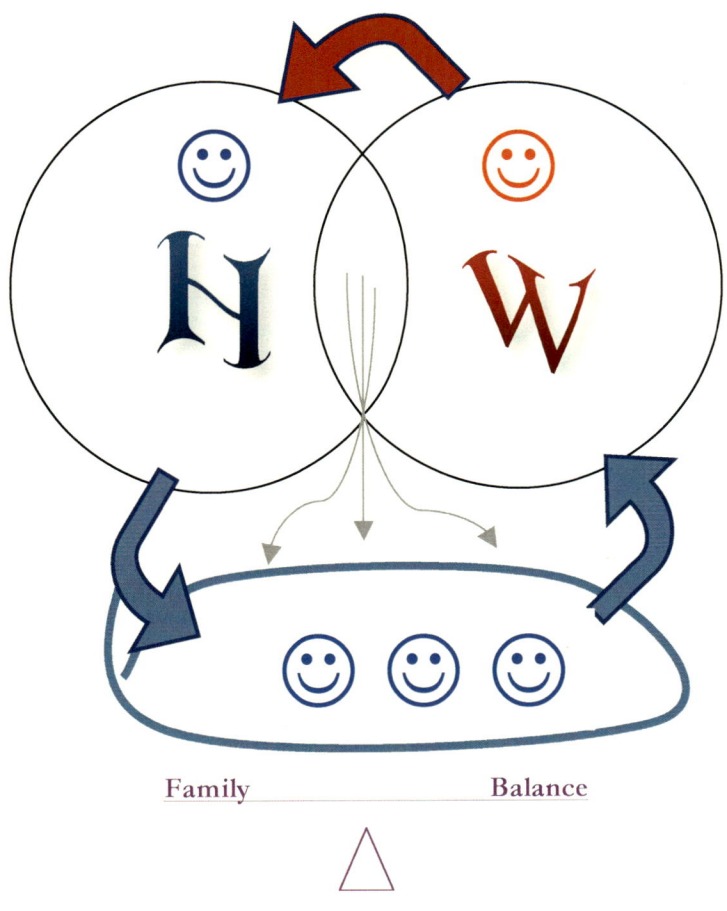

Family   Balance

And the children will better know what a loving marriage means for when they get married.

If you don't have your marriage, you don't have a family.

Children are better when parents are better. They are not

so good when Mom and Dad's marriage is not so good. Parents are the biggest influence of a child's life and this carries with them for their adult life and into their own marriage. Oh what a gift to give!

My father once told me about a time when he and my mom were flying back from Florida and a wife was showing affection to her husband while their two-year-old daughter was sitting on their lap. She kissed her husband and their daughter's face lit up with a big smile.

Later, I was sharing this story with a colleague of mine and he then shared his own story about a time when he and his wife were hugging in the kitchen. As their four-year-old daughter was walking from the living room to her bedroom and saw her parents hugging, she came over and gave them both a big hug.

I've said to my mom, if you chose me over Dad I would not be happy. As much as children want attention, they like to see their parents together—and to see them treating each other in a loving way.

My second wife and I were watching a movie called Jerry Maguire (released in 1996). Staring Tom Cruise as Jerry Maguire—a sports agent and—Renee Zellweger as Dorothy Boyd—a single mom of a young boy, who worked for the same firm. In the movie, Dorothy Boyd was the only employee that spoke up to take Jerry's risky invitation and leave the agency to join him and start his own agency. Even though Jerry was fired, Dorothy was very inspired by Jerry's honesty and integrity in a letter he wrote to his boss. As the movie progressed, Jerry grew fond of Dorothy and her little boy (who was very cute, fun, and looked up to Jerry). You could see the relationship building. For those who remember the movie, the famous lines of this movie are quoted as "*I love you…you complete me*" (said by Jerry to Dorothy in the living room surrounded by friends and family). She replied by saying: "*You had me at hello.*"

There was a scene, late in the movie, where Jerry was playing and having fun with her little boy, who was maybe five or six, and I said to my former wife, "Did you know that when a husband loves his children he is loving his wife?" She looked at me with a big affirming smile, as if saying to herself, *He's got it!*

Then I said, "Did you know that when a wife loves her husband she is loving her children?"

I looked over and she was tearing up—a shock, because she was not one to cry.

She asked, "Did you say that to hurt me? You really hurt me."

I reassured her, "No, I was just saying that as a general statement."

It was at this moment that my insight was strengthened to how true these two statements were.

"When a husband is loving his children, he is loving his wife."
"When a wife is loving her husband, she is loving her children."

Some husbands understand that loving their children is what makes the family tick. Most moms naturally place a high importance on the children, by design, and they like it when their husband shares the parenting.

Yet what is surprisingly unknown, by most women, is that *when a wife is loving her husband, she is loving her children*. My mom has told me that she didn't realize this until I shared it with her. Prior to children, women show their husband how important he is. They spend time together and he feels important (valued). Admittedly, men don't usually think in the pathway of loving the children as their default way to loving their wife. Most men want to love their wife directly, which can put stress on their wife because her priority is often for the children. It can be quite the mysterious disconnect.

From my research of surveying thousands of men and women, it has become apparent that these two statements alone could be considered the most insightful pieces of knowledge one can take from this book.

The part of this entire concept that I want to highlight the most, however, is the autopilot fear-based response that tends to occur as a result of a husband's or wife's unmet primary need. Women attack or reject when they feel their security is threatened, and men retreat when they feel insignificant or unimportant to the one they love. This seems to go around and around—it's these two fear-based responses that I've discovered to be the single biggest reason why marriages break down.

This happens in every marriage or serious relationship between men and women. It's even more amplified and prevalent in relationships that have lots of childhood and relationship baggage. The fear just keeps going around and around, and we need to be aware, get help, and start to make the change from fear to loving one another.

Husbands and wives have been struggling with understanding each other and selfish thinking for thousands of years. It seems like our expectations are high for our mate and not so high for ourselves. There are some great books and marriage programs available to us, but do we take the time to learn and practice? Usually, no. Doing the same thing over and over and expecting different results isn't the answer—in fact, it's Einstein's very definition of insanity. Before you can make things better, you need to stop making things worse. It takes understanding, discipline, and desire to make things better.

When parents are making their relationship a priority and loving one another, it ripples out to the children. We've heard the old saying that it takes a small village to raise a child—so, when a husband and wife are working together and loving one another, it makes for a better environment for the children. Yet, when moms and dads say, "My kids mean everything to me," I get concerned. Do they realize how important their spouse and marriage is?

Children need to see the love their parents have for each other and how they work together (e.g., showing patience, resolving conflict, forgiveness, building trust, etc.). Some parents say that if their marriage isn't working out, then maybe they should split. This is a cop-out. It may seem like the easy way out, yet in the long run this is damaging. I can speak from personal experience and have seen the destructive effects of divorce on families. Getting the marriage back on track and loving each other will be way better for all involved.

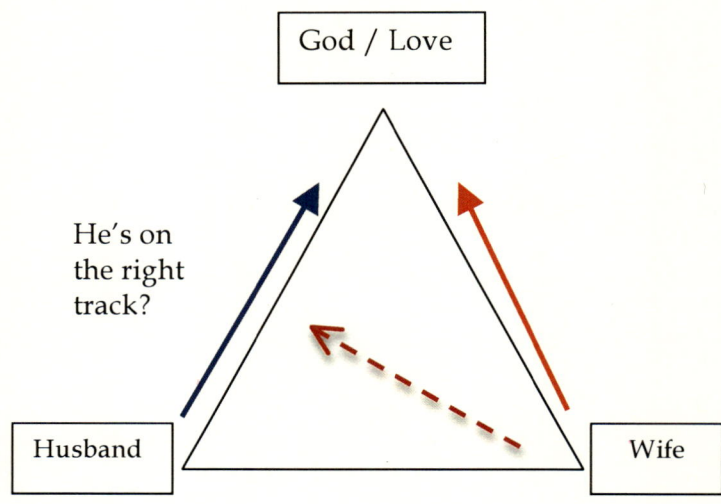

He's on
the right
track?

God / Love

Husband

Wife

Are you on the Right Track?

A woman is a barometer of a man's character—
she is watching her man. She looks for integrity, purpose,
work ethic, confidence, kindness, and strength that goes
the distance and doesn't give up. Okay, and good looks,
too. Typically, a woman knows and cares if her man is on
the right track in life. Yes, women may want the edgy and
spontaneous guy at times.

Yet, overall, a woman wants a man that has those

basic, reliable values and character traits—and that he values his wife in their relationship and the family. He is to be a One Woman Man. She wants to be able to count on his word and his actions. He is dependable, honest, and responsible. He'll be there. He'll be her rock. He'll sacrifice his selfishness for her needs and for the children.

When a man is on the right track and pointed in the direction of God's love, he lives out the qualities she's looking for. When he is off track, she knows it, and her gauges (feelings, insecurities, and actions) will let him know. Sometimes it doesn't come out so nice—yes, she may attack or reject. When a man is loving his wife in the way he was designed, he is courageous, patient, kind, and a man of integrity. He keeps working and persevering. He's there for her no matter what.

In Mark Gungor's book, he says a father has a high impact on the character that a family follows, while a mother usually has a higher impact on the nurturing aspect of the family. This is not always the case in all families. There are times where the roles of parents are somewhat different. Also remember, with single parenting it presents additional challenges. No matter what, a husband and wife are a team—they are not in competition.

I said to my cousin a few years ago, "Put your daughter on your shoulder. When that pop-up on your computer or phone appears, she is watching. When you are shaking hands and making a business deal, she is listening. When you are talking with your wife, she is watching and listening. Would she be pleased with her father's character?"

He said, "Thank you, I never thought about it that way, that means a lot."

Fathers are important to their sons' and daughters' lives. Mark Gungor has an audio program called *Men Matter*. Rick Johnson has a book called *That's My Girl*. Michelle Watson has a book called *Dad, I Really Need You*. All of these authors and speakers are highly respected and influential in the field of family and marriage counseling, and it's a testament to the truth of men's importance in the lives of their children that all of these materials exist and are so popular. It's unfortunate that much of our society has degraded the tremendous value of both men and women—as well as the family. Many TV programs have shown this gradual trend of lowering the bar.

I experienced this in my own childhood and have seen it in so many families. If fathers were more engaged in their children's lives, and in a way they needed, I believe more families would be together and there would be far fewer divorces.

It's important to recognize how integral your spouse is to the health and wellbeing of your family as a whole. When we recognize each other's value, we'll treat each other with more love and understanding.

Men's greatest need is for significance. By meeting your husband's need to feel significant to you, and by showing him and telling him how important he is, you reaffirm his commitment to the family. Women's greatest need is for security. When you meet your wife's need for security by showing and telling her that you are committed to taking care of her and the kids, you make her feel safe enough to rely on you and show you love. The single greatest reason that marriages break up is that husbands and wives fail to meet each other's greatest need, and this leads to a vicious cycle of attack or rejection and retreat. If we want a loving, healthy, stable family, it's imperative that we recognize our spouse's greatest need so that we can avoid that cycle. Remember, when a man is loving his children, he is loving his wife—and when a wife is loving her husband, she is loving her children.

CHAPTER SIX

UNDERSTANDING

What makes you tick? Why does your husband or wife think, say, and do what they do? There are four main areas to learn about that can help us understand what makes us tick.

Gender: Men and Women have unique differences.

Personality: Each of us has a unique personality.

Upbringing: How we are raised plus family of origin has major influence on our thinking and behaviours.

Values and Beliefs: What is important to us and what we believe influences our thinking and behaviour, and therefore our lives.

These areas are not meant to pigeonhole people, but rather to show how unique we are as individuals. Each of these areas are intertwined and collectively make up our ways of thinking and behaving. It's ironic that we can be upset when someone doesn't see things our way or meet our expectations, when we each have such unique ways about us. And the benefit of being unique is the richness it brings to our relationships. Through helping each other and learning to harness and appreciate the complementary differences, our relationships will grow. We are designed to come together—for each other—in unity and community. When we *tick together, we stick together.*

Gender

Many books have been written to help us understand how men and women think and behave. By design, men and women are made to complete, not compete. Where he is weak, she is strong, and where she is weak, he is strong. They complement each other and provide what each other needs and their children need. The parents' relationship impacts the children. The children's identity is found in their parents. They are half dad and half mom.

MAN'S brain

Men tend to think in boxes

WOMAN'S brain

Women tend to think in a big ball of wire

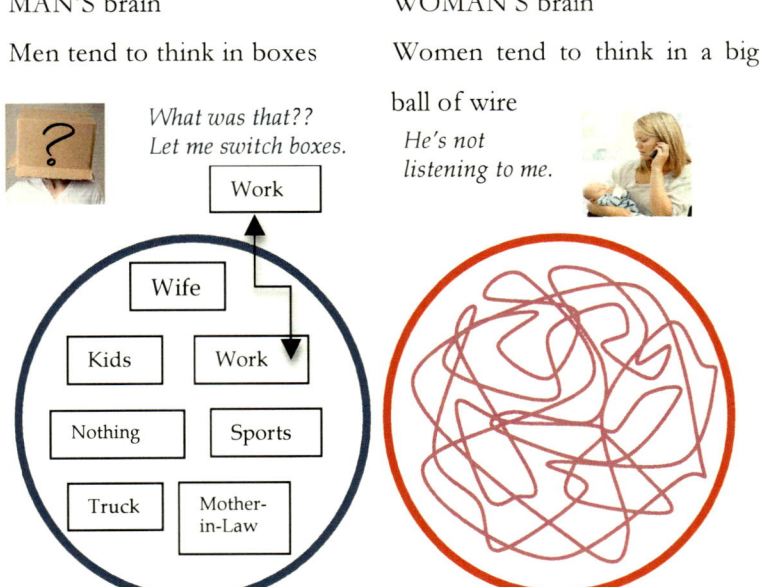

What was that??
Let me switch boxes.

He's not
listening to me.

Men pull out that box, think on that box, and then put that box back, making sure not to touch any other boxes. Often their favorite box is their *nothing box*. Generally, men have been practicing one thing at a time and thus practicing blocking other stuff out. Women, everything is connected to everything—husband, children, work, school, house, friends, etc., like a computer screen with 20 pop-up windows and she can't close any of them—only minimize them. Generally, women have been practicing paying attention to many things, especially when they become moms. Changes happen in mom that dad doesn't quite get. Is it *nature* or *nurture*? I believe it's both.

There are many writers that say this in different ways yet generally say the same thing. This example is largely taken from Mark Gungor's book, *Laugh Your Way to a Better Marriage*.

Every decision we make is tied to emotion. A psychologist once explained to me that a woman has six decision centers and one control center. The control center can suppress emotion. She's suppressing emotion much of the time, as to keep her emotions from taking over. She has six decision centers she has to control. A man has one decision center and one control center. He still has emotions to suppress, but only those from the one decision center (more singular in nature).

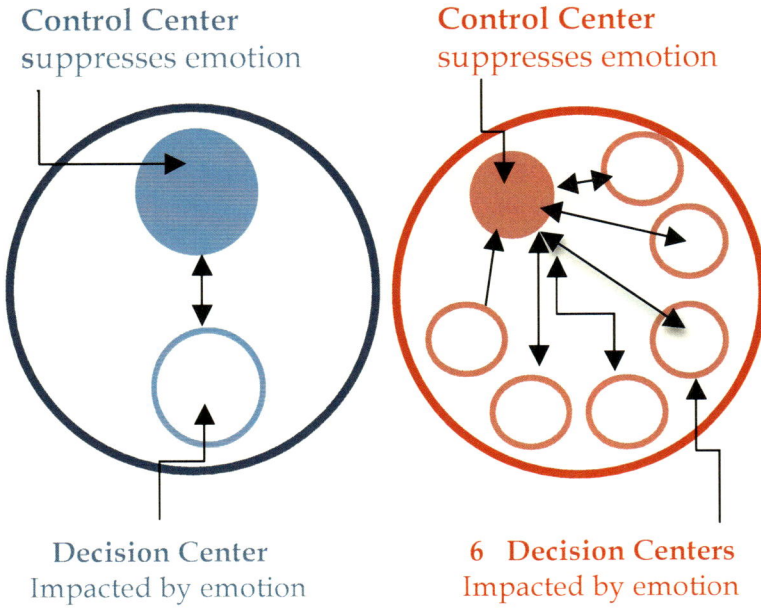

Control Center
suppresses emotion

Decision Center
Impacted by emotion

Control Center
suppresses emotion

6 Decision Centers
Impacted by emotion

Men tend to think more singular in action, blocking out other things to focus on one thing. While women tend to focus on many things, paying attention to the overall family needs. If it was left to most dads to raise the children, they may be living on macaroni, have diaper rash, and be playing computer games. Speaking from experience, haha. I've seen it the other way too.

We can see how different, yet complementary, men and women are when we learn and see the benefits of each other's qualities.

Completers *not* Competers.

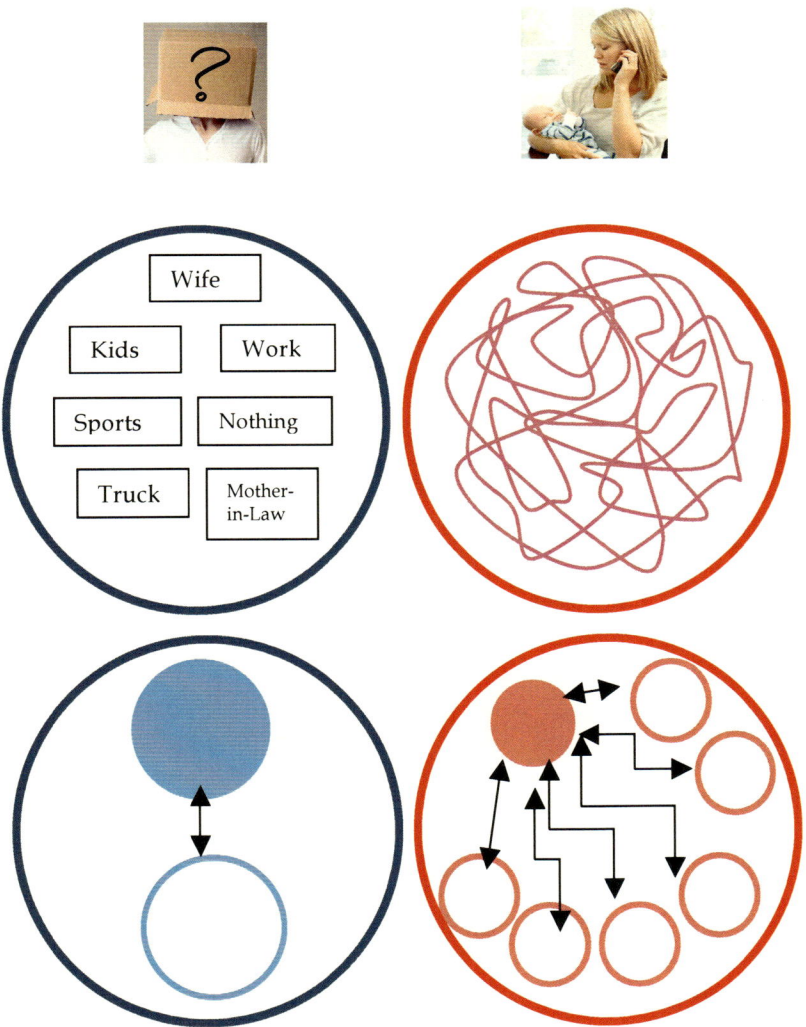

Family _____ Balance

Husband & Wife – Complete *not* Compete

Husband and Wife are the greatest team between two human beings (by design). The children need both mom and dad to learn what parenting and marriage is about. If dad and mom don't teach their children the right model of love in their marriage, who's going to do it? We need to recognize, appreciate, and harness each other's uniqueness, for a balanced and united marriage and family.

There are many books and researchers that explain the differences in male and female brains. In a February 2nd, 2011, John Wiley and Sons Inc. article, Michael Gurian explains how neurobiologists have shown over a hundred differences between the male and female brain. For example, females have more active brains by about 15 to 20 percent. Neither is inferior or superior, yet they work differently. Boys have more gray matter and less white matter than girls.

This allows the male brain to focus on one thing by compartmentalizing (like thinking in *boxes*). The female brain has more white matter and this allows her to move activity throughout the brain (left and right). It tends to allow her brain to focus on more things at a time, and less on one thing at a time. As I was taking my certification on brain-based thinking and behaviors through Emergenetics International, I was also shown similar information about the unique differences between male and female brain activity.

Gurian states that the gray matter acts like a neurotransmitter which compartmentalizes and localizes the activity in a single place (e.g., in an aggressive part of the brain) rather than spreading the activity to other parts of the brain. While the white matter, more prevalent in the female brain, networks activity to different parts of the brain, including emotion and empathy. As well, the male brain goes to rest more often than a female's brain. This can cause their attention towards activities, relating to others, and emotions to react differently. Maybe that's why Mark Gungor's book says men have a "nothing box" and that they like to go there more often to retreat or regroup.

For example, how many women say to their man, "You haven't heard a word I just said, have you?" Sorry gents—it happens.

Either way we know the male and female brains have unique activities and ways of behaving. It's been said that boys tend to be more spatial and girls more relational.

Okay, maybe that's why men are often out in space some where. The male brain, especially the right hemisphere, has more neural centers that cause them to focus on how objects move in space (how things move, where they are located, and how they fit). Where females then tend to be more focused on relational and verbal activity. This is not to say females are not spatial or males are not relational, yet from my own experience of my children and seeing my grandson, I can better understand what makes them tick and how they behave—it's very cool!

My counsellor once said, "Most men are relational misfits." I don't think all men are relational misfits. However, they do tend to relate differently than women. I believe men have a significant role as the relational model in the marriage and the family. Many men may not be overly sensitive and can tend to be more logical. Yet this is not always the case, in fact there are some shifts in various demographics today—as you will see in the next chapter, when I cover personality types. Gender is only partially responsible for how men and women think, feel, and behave.

For now, I want to share some insights about what I have learned and experienced regarding men needing to see the responsible impact they have on shaping their marriage and family.

In Steve Farrar's book *Point Man* there is a chapter called "Save the Boys." Since the industrial revolution, fathers went from working on the family farm to working away in the factories. Work ethic, values, character, and teaching their children were relegated to the backburner. And less time equals less influence. How do you spell love to a child? T-I-M-E.

My first piece of insight and advice is for men to *stay* in the fire—to never quit on his family. And he needs to stay engaged and be there for his wife and children. Marriage isn't always on fire, but when it gets rough, husbands need to stay and not let feelings of rejection from their wife keep them from persevering. Retreating and quitting do not help your wife's (or girlfriend's) need for security. If you're not man enough to handle her emotions, where is she going to go? She may look to someone else to fill that void. One of the fellows I was coaching asked me, "Can I tell my wife, *that when a wife loves her husband, she is loving her children?*" I said no. He looked at me with a big *why* on his face.

Listen guys, I have messed this up big time. Telling your wife what to do usually comes across as preaching or criticizing. It sounds like you're superior which makes her feel inferior. Most guys feel the need to *fix* problems. Most men think, "Why are we talking unless we are solving a problem?" Most women think, "Why are we solving a problem—I just want you to listen." Oops! Solving *isn't* listening. She wants to be understood not fixed.

When a man gives compassion and understanding to his wife it shows that he cares. A woman usually knows if her man is on the right track. Women admire and appreciate a man that is patient, kind, hard working, honest, forgiving, confident, focused, and purposeful. Sorry gents, it's a tall order but it's important.

Rejection is a common struggle for guys. Most guys let ego and pride get in the way. They don't realize how things get so mixed up until it gets to be a big problem. Often they check out. This can be true for wives too.

I want to let wives know that your man is concerned about what you and his peers think of him. I have struggled in my life with checking-out. Some men will pour themselves into their work or some bad choices when their marriage or family life isn't going so well. This can make it worse.

I want to let husbands know that the feelings of abandonment your wife may have can cause her to think you don't care about her or the family. If you want to see your wife reject you more or nag you more, then just keep working longer hours or watching more television or spending more time on the computer—more time away from the family. Men, you know in business and sports it's about going through the tough stuff and not avoiding it or abandoning it. Your wife and children need your *perseverance* and *time*. If you want a super woman you need to be a super man.

The following are what I believe to be the greatest ways a husband can love his wife and a wife can love her husband. In combination with the rest of this book, understanding these ways to love your spouse can help rebuild your relationship.

For men, loving your wife when you have been attacked or rejected, and *staying* in the fire with love for her, is one of the most important things you can do— never give-up. Even though she says or shows you that she wants nothing to do with you, it's not what she is really feeling in her heart. I know this is confusing, but it is more than likely the case. Looking past the wrongs and the hurtful behaviour and seeing her pain and need for love is the only way to let her know she is safe and that you will never leave her, no matter what. Remember, hurt people tend to hurt people, and being able to forgive and see past the behaviour is key to your unconditional love.

For women, loving your husband is *believing* in him and letting him know you need him, desire him, and admire him, even when you feel abandoned. When his tank is empty, he needs your fuel—your love and cheerleading. Not that you are begging in a needy way but in a loving and affectionate way—caring about him and your relationship. Also realize that when you attack him or reject him, his reaction may be to retreat because he is not feeling good about himself. Please don't take this as him abandoning you. Take this as a clue that you need to let him know how important he is to you. Your man wants to be your hero, yet can really struggle with how or knowing what to do at times. He needs to know when and how he is doing with words of appreciation or physical affection. He needs to know what you like and need.

This is a life-long journey of togetherness, communication, and growth. It takes time with an invested heart and mind over the long haul. The richness comes along the way. *When a man treats his wife like a queen and a woman treats her husband like a king they make a great team.*

PERSONALITY

A good friend of mine asked my 23-year-old son one time a cool question. Instead of asking him the usual, "What do you do?" He asked my son, "What makes you tick?"

Think about this question for a minute. What makes you tick? My guess is that most people don't even think about what makes themselves tick. Many of us may not really know.

My son answered in a split second, "I like fun."

Largely, our society says I'm defined by *what I do, what I have* and *what others think about me.* This last one seems so significant. We worry about this one—I'm not good enough, wanted, or accepted for who I am— especially by those close to me.

I was quite amazed at how accurately and with certainty my son answered this question. He was bang-on. I think it's taken much of my life to know what makes me tick. I am proud of my son and the growth he gained through some tough times. His childlike honesty was nice to see. It's too bad we can lose this honesty and often chase the all-status race—which turns out to be plastic and phoney.

My friend replied, with a laugh and a big smile, and said, "When I was 18, my middle name was F–U–N."

There's not one person that is identical to another. My kids and other family members have filled out their personality assessments and it is awesome to see how unique they are. It's quite amazing how their personality profile rings true to their thinking and behavioural preferences.

My personality points to why I have written this book and why I study the relationship between man and woman. I am very relational, sensitive, and analytical. Some guys like to study engines or structural designs. Me, I like to study people, with a passion for creating positive and caring relationships. I believe relationships are the most important and the most challenging aspect of life—and undoubtedly worth the investment of our time, understanding, and patience.

We are all similar, yet we are also different. It'd be a boring world if we were all the same. Nor would we learn how to grow in our relationships if we didn't have to work at it with different perspectives, qualities, and behaviours. Introvert or extrovert, we are all wired for unity. The very core of our humanity comes from uniting man and woman.

When I had my manufacturing company, my friend introduced me to the True Colors System. I hired a consultant to come and facilitate some training within our company and the fun began. My belief was, and my experience showed, that most organizations treat you like a number. When raising equity funds from investors to start my company, the final tag line of my presentation was: *"When people feel good about who they are and what they are doing, it's way better."*

I wanted people to know they were more important than the product or any mistakes we made. I believed that if we could understand each other, we could better accept each other's differences and perspectives. We could also harness the collaborative qualities that each one brought to the table. The performance of a company always flows from its people. However, many give lip service to the importance of their people and put too much emphasis on the performance or the money at the expense of their people. I knew that a manufacturing plant with a few hundred people working in close quarters and tight time lines would have its challenges. Mistakes, misunderstandings, conflicts, gossip, and blaming would be better managed with a workplace that valued people first and united the team. Patience, forgiveness, and honesty can be a big challenge in the workplace. Building trust and understanding was key, and knowing each other's personality helped us to have some fun and relate better to each other. It helped me to know how to motivate people I cared about.

We also brought spouses and partners in to do the personality assessment. I wanted them to feel like they were a part of the team and know we wanted relationships at home to be better as well. From my years of coaching hockey, I knew building positive chemistry was way better—not just being a number.

There are many systems to understand personality and human behaviour, such as: True Colors, Meyers

Briggs, DISC, Emergenetics, Animal Characters, Carl Jung, Hippocratic theory and various others. Here's a quick look at some of these that may help you to better understand your own personality and that of your spouse.

True Colors:

Orange	Blue	Gold	Green
Spontaneous	Sensitive	Structured	Analytical
Risk taking	Compassion	Organized	Solving
Lime Light	Affection	Responsible	Logical
Optimistic	Harmony	Consistent	Inquisitive
Performance	Romantic	Respect	Competence
Fun/Play	Dream	Loyal	Accuracy

DISC

Dominance	Influencing	Steadiness	Compliance
Decisive	Inspiring	Consistent	Dependent
Demanding	Convincing	Passive	Systematic
Ambitious	Sociable	Deliberate	Diplomatic
Competitive	Trusting	Patient	Cautious
Venturesome	Warm	Resists Change	Accurate

Hippocrates, According to Wikipedia:

Sanguine temperament is traditionally associated with air.

People tend to be lively, sociable, carefree, talkative, and pleasure-seeking. They can make new friends easily, be imaginative and artistic, and often have many ideas. They can be flighty and changeable; thus sanguine personalities may struggle with following tasks all the way through and be chronically late or forgetful.

Choleric temperament is traditionally associated with fire. People tend to be egocentric and extroverted. They may be excitable, impulsive, and restless, with reserves of aggression, energy, and passion and try to instill that in others. They tend to be task-oriented and getting a job done now. They can be ambitious, strong-willed, and like to be in charge. They can show leadership, are good at planning, and are often practical and solution-oriented. They appreciate receiving respect for their work.

Melancholic temperament is traditionally associated with the element of earth. People may appear serious, introverted, cautious, or even suspicious. They can become preoccupied with the tragedy and cruelty in the world and are susceptible to depression and moodiness. They may be focused and conscientious. They often prefer to do things themselves, both to meet their own standards and because they are not inherently sociable.

Phlegmatic temperament is traditionally associated with water. People with this temperament may be inward and private, thoughtful, reasonable, calm, patient, caring, and tolerant. They tend to have a rich inner life, seek a quiet, peaceful atmosphere, and be content with themselves. They tend to be steadfast, consistent in their habits, and thus steady and faithful friends.

Myers-Briggs

The following has been taken from the Myers & Briggs Organization's official website: The purpose of the Myers-Briggs Type Indicator® (MBTI®) personality inventory is to make the theory of psychological types described by C. G. Jung understandable and useful in people's lives. Perception involves all the ways of becoming aware of things, people, happenings, or ideas. Judgment involves all the ways of coming to conclusions about what has been perceived. If people differ systematically in what they perceive and in how they reach conclusions, then it is only reasonable for them to differ correspondingly in their interests, reactions, values, motivations and skills. If people differ in what they perceive and in how they reach conclusions (Judgment), then it can make a difference in their interests, behaviors, thinking, values, abilities and motivation. Do you prefer to focus more outwardly or more inwardly? Do you tend to see the basic information or do you prefer to interpret and add meaning. There are sixteen basic personality types in Meyers-Briggs inventory, plus additional sub classifications.

	Subjective	Objective
Deductive	iNtuition or Sensing	Perception or Judging
Inductive	Feeling or Thinking	Introversion or Extroversion

ISTJ	ISFJ	INFJ	INTJ
ISTP	ISFP	INFP	INTP
ESTP	ESFP	ENFP	ENTP
ESTJ	ESFJ	ENFJ	ENTJ

The bottom line is that human behavior really hasn't changed since the beginning of mankind. Different labels and descriptions have been studied and presented over thousands of years. Why? Because relationships have always been very important to us and understanding how we behave and treat each other offers some real benefit. I also believe human beings are designed to search for their identity and they like to know who they are and who others are—especially those we are close to.

My focus and familiarity is with the 4 colors developed and labeled in 1972 by True Colors (Don Lowry). I've also studied other types of assessment tools. I find the four colors (Blue Green Orange Gold) straightforward, personal, easy to remember and use. It's no less complex or accurate. Understanding one's personality—or one's spouse's, or co-worker's, or family member's—is important. It can help bridge the gap towards better relationships. The book *Men are from Mars and Women are from Venus* as well as the book called *Men are Waffles and Women are Spaghetti* tend to put men and women into two different categories, even though they recognize, not all men and women belong strictly to the two generalizations. This is why I have included Personalities, Upbringing, and Values & Beliefs, along with Gender, to more fully understanding ourselves and each other.

True Colors:

Men (appx. 50–70%)	**Women** (appx. 50–70%)
Orange (or Green)	Blue (or Gold)
Green (or Orange)	Gold (or Blue)
Gold	Orange
Blue	Green
Often Blue is in their last two	Often Green in their last two
Usually Orange or Green will be in their top two.	Usually Blue or Gold will be in their top two.

 Blue: Sharing, Sensitive, Compassionate, Relational, Romantic, Harmony, Supportive, Encouraging, Sympathetic, Intuitive, Feelings, Likes Affection, Affectionate, Caring.

Green: Solving, Analytical, Research & Study-it, Comparing, Fixing, Why, Perfectionist, Accuracy, Efficiency, Debating, Likes Facts and Proof.

Orange: Spontaneous, Fun, Likes the Limelight, Decisive, Risk-taking, Gamer, Active, Variety, Networks & Socializes, Upbeat, Wing-it.

Gold: Structure, Organized, Plans, Lists, Responsible, Loyal, Duty, Schedule, Makes Sure, Thinks of Consequences, Respectful.

The majority of male and female personalities often show some specific and opposite differences. Not all men and women fit in two buckets. With True Colors and the scale I use, there are more than 900,000 unique combinations. I would suggest that in the last generation or so the stats have changed somewhat. I believe that the prevalence of more broken families has significantly impacted our thinking, behaviours, and beliefs.

That said, you'll often see that *opposites attract*. So even if a man or woman doesn't fit the majority, they will likely be attracted to one who is fairly opposite and complementary to their own personality. For example, if you are more of a talker, then you will likely be attracted to someone who is more of a listener.

The other reason why I believe opposites tend to be attracted to each other, by design, is for the benefit of raising the children—they offer the balanced blend the children need. Children can have quite a mix or opposite personalities to that of either parent. Is it nature or nurture? The term *nature* can be viewed as a blueprint. The term *nurture* can be viewed as parenting or upbringing. As a parent, I wanted to raise my children equally, as best as I could. But no matter what, they each had their own unique personality. So many factors play into how our children are wired and how they grow. Sometimes parents can try too hard to force their children—thus living vicariously through them. It's hard and we want the best for them. Knowing their personality and being engaged in their lives can really help bring out the best in our children.

I've assessed a number of children's personalities using True Colors. As well, I know many schools use it extensively to help with understanding, motivating, and teaching children. Understanding you and your spouse's personality, plus your children's, can really help you improve your parenting and your marriage. A key to unconditional love is accepting, and understanding helps us to better accept.

By better understanding, we can start to

answer some age-old questions, like: Why can wives seem overly sensitive? Why can men be so cold or have such a temper? Why does she want to talk so much? Why won't he share his thoughts and feelings? Why doesn't he listen to what I'm saying? Why does she divert her attention when I'm explaining? Why is she all over the map? Why is he so single-minded?

These types of questions can run through our mind and drive us crazy. However, we can choose to care, understand, and build bridges—or to be ignorant, selfish, and divided. Such perspectives may be reversed. But, when you understand your spouse's wiring, you can begin to accept and love them in a way that meets their needs.

UPBRINGING

Upbringing is related to family of origin, but family of origin also goes back into previous generations—which has a significant influence on the effects of nature and nurture on children. It is wise for all of us to become aware of our parents and their patterns. It can help us understand ourselves—the good and the not so good. Forgiveness and working on the healthy changes is important. I would strongly recommend Dr. Caroline Leaf's book *Switch On Your Brain*, to help retrain the thinking and emotional channels in our mind. As she says, "It's mind over matter." To change our mind takes time, devoted mental work, and knowing that God loves us and is always with us. He is our hope and we can trust Him to work in our life.

Being loved is the most powerful motivation human beings have. Our ability to love is often shaped by our experiences. *We usually love others as we have been loved.* Think about how you love those close to you and how you treat or think about others. Think about how you love your spouse and how your spouse might like to be loved.

How do those two ways compare? Do you even know how those two ways compare?

At birth, all of a baby's organs—with the exception of the brain—are fully developed. At birth, a baby's brain has more than 100 billion cells. Some are already connected for the heart to beat and the lungs to breath, yet most brain cells are formed after birth, within the first few months and years. These connections shape a baby's feelings, thoughts, and behaviours.

A child's brain is largely developed before school age. And it's the childhood years that greatly shape one's foundation for healthy relationships.

Pressure from our parents, siblings, and peers about our performance and appearance has a huge impact on how we see ourselves. It can be damaging or enriching. Unfortunately, we determine our identity by what others think of us.

Roughly 90% of our thinking and behaviours are non-cognitive (e.g., subconscious). For the most part, we are on auto-pilot (habits, programing, and wiring). If 90% is auto-pilot (subconscious) then roughly 10% is conscious. It's the conscious that is responsible for filtering, selecting, and receiving what goes into our subconscious. And it's the conscious part that we are able to control. What we think on and what we do is critical. However, it's up to the parents to create the loving environment that a child will receive, for they have not developed the consequential thinking in the frontal lobe yet. The frontal lobe is largely developed in the teen and young adult years.

An article, by Anne-Laura van Harmelen and Marie-José van Tol on brain development shows the affect of emotional maltreatment in childhood. In this article, they explain how early brain development is the foundation of human adaptability and resilience. They talk about how positive and negative experiences greatly affect brain development at such a young age. They say children are especially vulnerable to persistent negative influences and how significant positive experiences have a huge impact on the child's life for achievement, success, and happiness.

They say the first three years of a child's brain has

up to twice as many synapses as it will have in adulthood, and this means they are very sensitive to absorbing external influences at very young ages. They state: "Between conception and age three, a child's brain undergoes an impressive amount of change. At birth, it already has about all of the neurons it will ever have. It doubles in size the first year, and by age three it has reached 80 percent of its adult volume. (*Urbanchildinstitute.org*)

They explain that children who are maltreated by parents or carers (in the form of verbal abuse, being humiliated, or not being shown affection) have an increased risk of depression or anxiety disorders in adulthood. Their research showed how emotional abuse was just as harmful as physical abuse with regard to the possible link between emotional abuse and a reduction in the volume of the medial pre-frontlal cortex. This is the part of the brain that plays an important role in our emotional behavior and how we handle stress. A reduction in this area of the brain could explain why adults who have suffered emotional abuse have an increased risk of developing depression and anxiety disorders.

These researchers have found similar findings related to the effects of more visible forms of child abuse, such as physical or sexual abuse. I share this article only to show how significant the treatment of a child is to their adult life, and how important loving care is to our brains. Our upbringing, and family of origin, has a huge impact on our lives. Fear of so many things, that we aren't even aware of, begins in our early years. Fears can keep us from making healthy changes. Fears affect how we see ourselves and how we see and treat others.

Not only I have I seen this in my life, I have seen it in the lives of others close to me. Many of us desperately want connection, acceptance, and approval that seemed lacking in childhood. *FEAR* stands for: *F*alse *E*vidence *A*ppearing *R*eal. Yet, the opposite, Love and Faith, cast out fear.

If someone hurts you out of fear, then to forgive them is the right and healthy thing to do. Returning the hurt or judgement only brings more fear in both of you. Anything that is not of love and faith is of fear. *Revenge may be sweet in the contemplation, yet painful in the aftermath.* Fear can be crippling and destructive. Often our adult behaviors are a manifestation of emotions related to our experiences of childhood and young adulthood. We tend to hear so many more negatives and criticisms than we do positive encouragement, especially from those closest to us. Parents, spouses, siblings, school friends, work colleagues, coaches, and teammates can say and do things that are hurtful, critical, and selfish. Relationships are challenging enough as it is. When there has been abuse or unhealthy treatment in our childhood, it has significant influences in our lives and relationships.

Lesley Maunder and Lorna Cameron also provide information and guidance for adults physically, emotionally or sexually abused as children. They share some quotes by people who have experienced abuse—a few are listed below. They also talk about *what abuse is,* and share how some people respond to the pain of past abuse.

"I have memories coming into my mind all the time of what happened to me when I was a child. I can't understand why. I've

never thought about those things until now... I don't like what I can remember, it fills me full of fear, I can't believe someone would do that to a child..."

"Relationships are a disaster area for me. I can't trust anyone...the same old pattern occurs again and again, especially with men. It is as if my dad was still around and still harming me. I even react the same, always trying to please and pretending there is nothing wrong...what is it about me that causes this?"

"I know I don't want to face what has happened in my life, so I don't. I drink, take drugs, binge, and starve. All of this hides what has happened..."

"I can never say no to anyone, they can walk all over me, do and say what they want. It's only later that I begin to feel angry and it's usually at myself..."

"I sometimes think I'm completely bad and rotten, then at other times I think no it's not me, it's them..."

They share how child abuse still goes on today and often is unrecognized. I believe it's a lot closer to home than we realize. Abuse comes in various forms: *Neglect*: emotional and/or physical. *Violence*: physically and/or emotionally (e.g., beating, biting, yelling, belittling, harsh criticism, blaming, and name calling). *Sexual*: Intercourse, fondling, and other inappropriate physical manipulation.

Abuse can be subtle or it can be forceful. It can be overtly damaging or manipulative in little ways that can have long-term effects. It can be over a short period of time or over a long time. It can be from parents, spouses, siblings, boyfriends, girlfriends, friends, teammates, teachers, coaches, work colleagues, school mates and strangers. Whatever the case, it's cruelty from one to another, even from ourselves. Those who have been abused may not even remember the hurtful times or relate the abuse to their current ways of handling stress or relationships. Many of us deny or dismiss past emotional hurts of abuse. I know for myself my escapes and coping manifested unhealthy choices and thinking patterns. As a child, I wasn't physically abused by my parents, but there was some neglect. Growing up, I was bullied, and as an adult I have been on the receiving and giving end of very hurtful treatment.

In Muander's and Cameron's article they share how some deal with emotions from abuse and what questions can be asked. Examples: Do I try to excuse it? What causes my stress or outbursts? Do I make light of it? (e.g., he bruised me but it didn't go any further, it was my fault, I must have done something wrong, I was only touched).

Those who are abused may struggle with some serious emotional and physical patterns (e.g., eating disorders, bedwetting, nightmares, lashing out, anger, hiding, cheating, depression, not wanting to work or engage with others). Some may have deep fears and anxiety, or have tried attempted suicide or self harm. Others jump from relationship to relationship using and abusing themselves and others.

The long-term effects are usually significant. When there has been abuse, it can cause us to feel unlovable and to withdraw, not wanting to risk letting others get too close. Being intimate and honest can be a real problem. Unhealthy sexual relationships can become a mask or way of coping with feeling unaccepted or not worthy.

I've seen and experienced how damaging and hurtful abuse can be—not only to the one who has been abused, but to the people in their lives. Some wind up being a rescuer, some an abuser or user, running from the fear of being honest or not knowing what to do. We all want to be loved and to love, yet how we go about it can make all the difference.

From the trials and heartbreaks of the past, I understand—and my prayers go out to you. You are worthy, you are loved, you are beautiful, just the way you are, and God loves you more than you could ever imagine!

VALUES & BELIEFS

Values and beliefs are tied to our upbringing, our personality, and how we treat one another. How we treat others and what we believe is right, good, and acceptable is largely rooted in what we were modelled growing up. Unfortunately, selfish behaviours and character are modelled more often than not, and thus practiced as acceptable and normal—passed on to the next generation. Criticism, neglect, and attacking have a huge impact on children and how they build relationships. If our values and beliefs are dishonouring, and not responsible or loving, we will reap what we sow.

Loving, believing, and choosing is foundational to who we are. What we believe is critical to the healthiness of our minds, our lives, and our relationships. Those who believe that God is love and that He created us to love one another may find that their beliefs differ from those who don't, or those who are not sure. Having faith in God and the love He has for us is a big step for many. Often, people want to believe in a greater power or a creator, yet societal norms can pull us in different directions and make us doubt.

What is more important than proving? *Believing.* We are Believing Beings. In fact, not believing, is *still* believing. No matter what, values and beliefs will play a big part in our relationships.

The more we have the same beliefs and values as our mate, the more aligned we are. This is foundational in marriage and to building a connected, satisfying relationship.

SUMMARY

As we've seen in this chapter of *Understanding*, there are four key factors that make up an individual. We are all unique human beings, yet we share many characteristics with those around us that allow us to sympathize with and relate to each other. Some of these traits that dictate much of our lives are based on our nature. Our *genders* shape part of who we are and how we experience life. *Personality*, too, plays a huge role in our thoughts and behaviors, as well as in how we perceive and treat others. Our *upbringing* and family of origin makes up most of our nurture experience in our early lives, and therefore has a big impact on shaping the person we turn out to be. Our interactions with our parents and their interactions with each other teach us about relationships and how to love one another. Negative experiences in our upbringing can leave us with trauma and pain that we'll need to work on throughout our lives. Our *values and beliefs* also play an important role in shaping who we are and who we want to be.

When we recognize how all of these factors have

influenced and shaped us, we can then better understand our own motives and behaviors. Understanding what drives us, and makes us tick, is the first step to being able to change unhealthy behaviors and habits. By recognizing the factors that have shaped our *spouse's* life experience and worldview, we also have the opportunity to exercise more compassion, love, and understanding toward them, which will strengthen our relationships.

Ask yourself: How do I relate to those around me? How do I relate to the one I love? Do I cherish the uniqueness and goodness of who they truly are?

CHAPTER SEVEN

COMMUNICATION

How many of us think the other person needs to hear what's in my head or how I'm feeling? Communication is key to any relationship. Miscommunication requires face-to-face or voice-to-voice interaction to resolve misunderstandings. Emails and texts tend to *start* misunderstandings, instead of resolve them—and then damage control is needed.

ADDICTED to the SCREEN

- ➢ 93% of communication is non-words
- ➢ We're getting good at the 7% but worse at the 93%
- ➢ We're trying to get the 93% connection from the 7% machine (and we don't even realize it)
- ➢ Technology can often result in communication that is impersonal and lacks honesty and emotional connection (and it's that connection that we are wired for and need)
- ➢ Very limited and partial and fragmented
- ○ hiding and avoiding are comfortable but harmful.

➤ Replacing face-to-face with ☺ to ☺ emoticons.

➤ Diminishing versus improving Relationships

We are so *connected* we are *disconnected*. Our *virtuality* is sadly substituting *reality*. So often we think it's about *information*, when really it's about *relation*.

If we were to cover our eyes to talk to each other, or cover our mouth, or turn our back, it doesn't work so good. We're wired to connect face-to-face and voice-to-voice. Face-to-Face lets someone know our sincerity. It can melt hearts and break down barriers. When we hide behind texting, it increases our fears and misunderstandings. The odd text for quick info or flirting can be okay, but best to keep it infrequent and not become a habit or taking the easy or impersonal way out.

  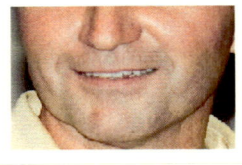

People get let go from their job via email. People break up relationships by texting because they're too scared to communicate in person. And we think texting and email-ing are better? The eyes are the door to the soul. A smile warms a heart. A hug says it's good to see you or lets you know I care.

I believe we're starving for connection, as we become more and more emotionally separated by the screen—*the screen between.* We might think we're connected more than ever before, but this is not the case. Our attention is simply more divided than ever before.

It's our focused and loving attention that our relationships need the most. When we keep going to the screen, it's like our air hose is being slowly cut off and we just keep sucking harder, even though we get less out. Without emotional connection, we're withering away. We may try to replace it with physical connection, but that doesn't fully cut it. We're wired for emotional connection and it takes courage to be emotionally open—which is diminished from behind the screen.

Here is an example: pretend you have a four-year-old child and you place your child into an enclosed glass room with a screen to watch. You can't go in and your child can't come out (no touch, no talk). You can walk by a few times a day, from outside the glass room, with a happy face emoticon and the words I love you on a piece of paper, but that's it. If you did this for six months, what do think is going to happen to your child? Your child and your relationship will become emotionally starved. They'll wither from neglect and lack of real, meaningful human interaction. What do you think we are gradually doing to our relationships by increasing our screen time instead of face time?

Our ability to relate, to be united, to belong, to love is so limited and fragmented by the screen. Yet, we habitually become more and more comfortable with being distant, isolated and lonely. The little hits of connection we get from the screen are often all we have to replace the meaningful connections we really need, but of course they can't possibly do so! It just makes us more lonely. Being lonely is a huge reason for depression, maybe the biggest!

We want to know, "Does someone want me?" We answer to the machine all day long. We're blinded by the quick hit and the instant gratification it provides. It's like drugs, it only lasts a little while and we go back for more. The more we practice, the more we crave it. We get tired of the phone, but we can't seem to escape it. We're creatures of habit, and sometimes it seems like the majority of our habits are bad ones.

I said to one young lady going up the escalator, "You don't have a cell phone in your hand!" She smiled. I said, "I tell girls it wrecks relationships."

She said, "It already has."

I said to another young lady, "You know what's better than texting?" She asked, "What?" I said, "Talking."

She replied as if she'd never considered this before, exclaiming, "That' so cool!"

In my view, it's one of the biggest habits and addictions of modern society. For many, more than 11 hours, and up to 17 hours per day a person is looking at a screen. The bulk of this is at our phone. Face-to-face and voice-to-voice communication is diminishing rapidly. So is our ability to have open, honest, emotionally connected relationships. When *da-face* in *da-phone* is our life, it's *da-structive*.

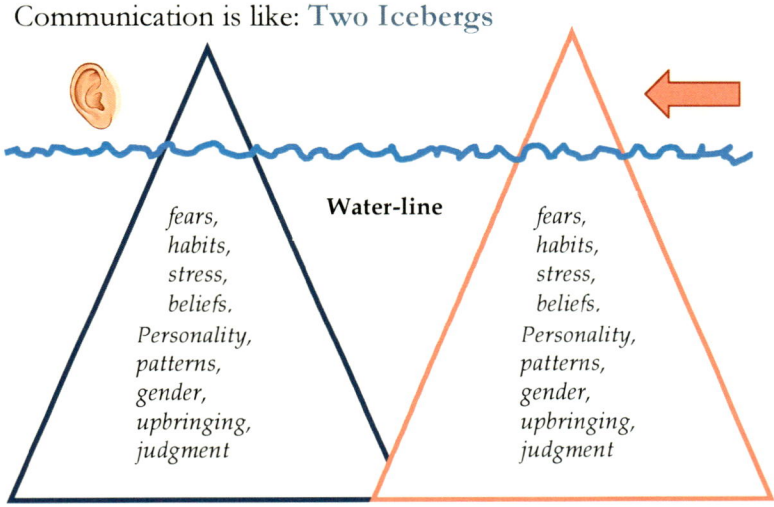

Communication is like: **Two Icebergs**

fears, habits, stress, beliefs. Personality, patterns, gender, upbringing, judgment

Water-line

fears, habits, stress, beliefs. Personality, patterns, gender, upbringing, judgment

This diagram shows two icebergs, which represent two people communicating. Above the waterline are the words spoken and what each other hears. Below the water line is a whole bunch of feelings, patterns, and stresses each person is dealing with or filtering information through while the conversation is going on.

Note: we can think about 400 words per minute. We speak about 100 words per minute. Yet we kick out only about 10 or 20 words to the other person when we are talking to them. We don't give them context to help them understand the 400 words per minute that are going through our head, we just expect them to know what we mean and follow along. As a friend of mine likes to say, with a little smile, "We're not mind readers, you know."

How much does our mind wander when someone is speaking? How many of us are waiting for our turn to talk and not hearing what the other person is saying? How many of us have filters, judgements, baggage, insecurities, and competitive thoughts (e.g., I'm right, they're wrong)?

What's the chance of sending and receiving with clarity or understanding on the first attempt? Likely very low. What's our expectation? Usually high — thus the frustration.

Communication breakdown is why misunderstandings happen — at home or at work. Emails and texts often start a misunderstanding. Emails are fine for recapturing what has been said and sending it out as notes for reference. Texts are fine for a quick piece of info or a picture. But to have meaningful conversation or to really feel connected, they can pose a problem.

Learning how to communicate, especially listening, is the key to a successful relationship. People want to feel understood and feel important, especially our spouse. Understanding comes from paying attention to the emotional content as much as or more than the words being spoken. This is how we are designed—here's proof.

A little four-year-old boy comes up to his mom while she is doing dishes and facing the window with her back towards her son. He is very excited to share something important with her.

"Mommy, Mommy, I want to tell you something!"

"Yes dear, what is it?"

He says, "No, Mommy, I want to tell you something!"

She continues facing the sink and the window. "I'm listening, dear…what is it?"

He says, "No, Mommy! I want to you to listen to me with your *eyes*."

How do you capture the most precious, funny, and personal moments with a few letters across the screen? You can't. Nothing beats being present in your own life and in your relationships.

The screen between us may seem easy, convenient,

and always accessible, but it results in a type of communication that is fragmented and impersonal. When will this merry-go-round of never-ending pseudo-connection give us a break? Help, I'm texting and I can't turn it off! I don't want it, but I'm addicted because it makes me feel like someone always wants me!

Our new-age definition of *talking* has become some key strokes on a screen. Relationships have been minimized to digits. There are two words in life we should pay heed to. One is bad, one is good. The bad word is *more* and the good word is *no*. Just say *no* to *more*. More is less…and less is more, after all. Less virtual is more real.

It has been claimed it takes between 43 and 62 muscles to frown and 17 to 26 to smile. When we make facial expressions, we're transmitting a packet of information that can be received, read, and interpreted. This isn't going to happen in a text, email, or *anti*-social media. We never really know if someone is sincere or what is going on behind the screen. Becoming comfortable with having conversations on the screen can create fears when important thoughts and feelings need to be expressed. We are creatures of habit, who have a predisposition to fear and find it *easy* to avoid tough conversations.

In these pictures, I see learning, I see security, I see adoration, I see looking up with trust. I see love in the faces of the mother, the father, and the child.

Love grows brains. *Listening is Loving.* When we listen to

understand it brings trust and connection. So how do we listen with a heart that wants to understand and care for each other? It's a mind shift and a heart shift to work on every day.

The Five Love Languages, by Gary Chapman, is an

amazing book about relationships and how to communicate our love to our spouse in a way that best fulfils their needs.

In it, Chapman suggests that each one of us contains within us what he calls a "love tank." This love tank needs to be refilled regularly and consistently for us to be happy and healthy and to feel like we are loved. When the tank is low, we feel unloved and unsatisfied. When the tank is full, we are brimming and overflowing with love! The tricky part is that not everyone's love tank can be filled the same way. What fills our tank depends on what *love language* we speak. Chapman posits that there are five possible love languages a person can speak. Those with the Affirmation language require sincere words of encouragement and verbal reassurances to know that our spouse loves us and to feel satisfied in our relationship. For those whose love language is Quality Time (conversation, activity, rest), we need our spouse to spend time with us, and be present and not distracted in order to feel valued and cared for. Those with the Acts of Service language like our spouses to perform concrete tasks like household chores to demonstrate their love. Those with the love language of Receiving Gifts need tangible proof that our loved one is thinking of us. And those whose primary language is Physical Touch need to be reassured that they are loved through physical actions, touch, and intimacy. Each of us speak one to two primary love languages. When our spouse speaks to us in *our* language, it fills our need for love. When we speak to our spouse in *their* language, it fills their tank. But, often, we don't speak the same primary love language as our spouse. If we don't take the time to learn what makes our spouse feel loved and valued, our relationship suffers and breaks down. That's why it's so important that we tailor the way we communicate with our spouse to our spouse's needs. The five love languages are outlined below:

Affirmation: Letting each other know you are important (words, emotion, physical) and you appreciate them. Believing in them so that they feel valued, safe, and wanted. Giving them words of encouragement, recognition, and support.

Quality Time: Sharing conversation, activity (work or play), or just relaxing together.

Acts of Service: Doing something for your partner. Something they would appreciate.

Gifts: It doesn't have to be expensive, but should be thoughtful, personal, homemade, or something they like.

Physical Touch: Holding hands, snuggling on the couch, hugs, kissing, back rubs, foot rubs, sensual caressing, flirting, playing around physically, sexual intimacy, sleeping together where there is some physical touch.

I suggest you read Gary's book and fully understand these love languages and how you can enrich your relationships.

As you can see, there are myriad ways to communicate with our spouses without the use of phones or computers! All communication needs to be sincere, caring, and honouring. Our motive is key. We are made to see and hear honesty and vulnerability—which that cannot be seen in a text.

There is a process for communicating, which I call *Safe Talk*. It allows the one sharing their feelings (sender) to the one listening (the receiver) to share in a very safe environment. It is a wonderful way of letting each other understand how the other feels without defensive remarks that causes tension, fear, and lack of trust. It confirms, affirms, and promotes understanding with empathy and compassion. It takes lots of practice, patience, and perseverance—but it is worth it!

Similar ways of communicating, I've experienced, are presented by Harville Hendrix, called Imago Therapy. As well, Retrouvaille, which uses a safe environment through writing to each other. Both ways can be difficult at first because the sender is risking their heart and facing fears of being judged or exposed to their loved one. This can be emotionally challenging, yet the invested time and effort can build trust and a loving connection. These and other similar ways of building caring communication have helped many couples rebuild their relationship.

We know that communication breakdown is a common response for why our relationships struggle, and it's true. But the motivation or, better yet, the motive of our heart is at the core of communication. The how is important, yet the why is more important. The *will* and the *want* make the *how* happen. *Motivation sustains perspiration.* Without a giving heart, it won't last.

CHAPTER EIGHT

A GIVING HEART

We all want to be heard. Some enjoy listening more than others, but many of us want to be heard, understood, and cared about. Am I a good friend to my spouse? Do I want the best for my spouse? How can I love my wife today? How can I love my husband in this moment? Do I take time to understand my spouse's thoughts, needs, and feelings? Or do I try and get my spouse to fit into what I want or the way I think? Am I controlling or caring? Do I seek to understand? Many of us may not consider that the *person* is more important than the topic.

Love is Patient: Patience is bitter but its fruit is sweet.

The dictionary defines Patience as: "The Quality of being patient in suffering," from Old French *patience*. "Patience; sufferance, permission," (12c.) and directly from Latin *patientia* "Patience, endurance, submission; quality of suffering," from *patientem* "To suffer, endure," from root *pei-* "To damage, injure, hurt" (see *passion*).

The opposite of patient is anxious—not wanting to wait. Impatient or anxious can take the form of quitting and not persevering. It tries to control or manipulate others. Persevering cannot happen without patience. Patience cannot happen without perseverance.

"Do not be anxious about anything, but in every situation, by prayer and petition, with thanksgiving, present your requests to God. And the peace of God, which transcends all understanding, will guard your hearts and your minds in Christ Jesus."
Philippians 4:6-7

I believe God's will and timing is better than anything I could imagine or orchestrate on my own. Why wouldn't I trust Him? Why would I pressure others? In relationships, it's often better to give someone space and let time apart create a desire to reconnect. It's good to build a friendship of slow growth. *You can't rush something that you want to last forever.*

You can't push a rope. Tug of war doesn't work.

Hang on to everything loosely and give people time—leave them with a memory of respect, kindness, and integrity. You'll never regret doing the right thing, even if others chose not to.

> *"Patience is not the ability to wait but how you act while you're waiting."* – Joyce Meyer

To me, it's also important to consider what I think about while I wait. Do I want the other person to know they are loved? Will I be available for them when they are ready to talk and connect?

It's inevitable that two people living in such close proximity as that of marriage will irritate each other. So if love is based on performance instead of patience, your marriage will only be as consistent as your spouse is *(love dare devotional)*. While being patient we can keep our thoughts on such things as these:

"Finally, my brothers and sisters, always think about what is true. Think about what is noble, right and pure. Think about what is lovely and worthy of respect. If anything is excellent or worthy of praise, think about those kinds of things."

– Philippians 4:8

Can you imagine if husbands and wives were more patient, kind, forgiving, and didn't quit on each other? I believe our marriages, families, communities, and our world would be stronger and more united.

"Patience is not the ability to wait but the ability to keep a good attitude (and my mouth shut) while waiting."

– Unknown

The sacrifice or suffering endured is worth the wait.

Love is kind:	Gentle, honest and considerate.
Love does not boast:	Love has humility.
Love is not proud:	Takes the first step towards making amends and being a friend.
Love is not rude:	Doesn't criticize, bully, or ignore.
Love is not self-seeking:	Sacrifice my wants for my spouse's welfare.
Love is not easily angered:	Attacking, harsh, and cruel treatment is fuelled by a practiced behaviour and stored-up victim feelings and thoughts.

Love keeps no record of wrongs:

Not revengeful or resentful. This doesn't mean we don't recognize the wrong. It means we don't hold bitter feelings or thoughts. Love always forgives. Grace builds bridges.

Love does not delight in evil, but rejoices with the truth:

> When we use someone, or hide, or run
> away—hoping it will go away, it does
> serious emotional damage to our wellbeing.

Love always protects:

> Protecting ties these points together.
> If I protect then I will not seek revenge, lie
> or cheat. I will not use someone for my gain.
> I will look for the good in that person. I will
> see them through God's eyes. I listen, serve
> and give a safe place.

Love always trusts:

> We want to trust and be trusted. Yet when
> trust is broken we struggle to trust again.
> Love keeps giving the other person a chance
> to rebuild that trust. We're not to find our
> validation or self-worth in another person. We are
> who God made us to be. We are fearfully and
> wonderfully made. Our trust is in Him because
> when we seek Him we know how much He loves
> us.

Love always hopes:

> Without hope there is no motivation to
> persevere. Ultimately our hope is in God.

Love always perseveres:

> Love never gives up. Hope and
> perseverance go together. The word
> *always* doesn't equal 99.9% it equals
> 100%. This is amazing love. This is
> a love that God has for us.
>
> *I can give what I know I have. I have God's love.*

MEN

Ask yourself, Is my wife important to me? Do I love to listen to my wife, because she is worth it?

When I see men letting their eyes and words wander in the direction of another woman, it bothers me. Not just because I feel bad for their wife, but because I can see how it affects him in the long term. A man that values himself will value his wife with integrity and compassion. I believe men are the relational model in the family and the marriage. I believe women look to a man they can respect and admire and feel secure with.

Looking back, I can see where I missed the mark big time. It's not easy to stay on track but it's worth it. Marriage is the greatest relationship and requires the greatest investment. Your wife and children are a gift to take care of and to love.

WOMEN

Ask yourself, Is my husband important to me? Do I believe in my husband, because he is worth it?

Today, many women are becoming more competitive and independent. In some ways, this is hurting the marriage and family. They are breaking away from marriages more than ever. Part of the reason for this is women have been treated poorly by men for hundreds and thousands of years. Yet, two wrongs don't make it right. "You go girl, you don't need a man!" You don't need to take that—move on. This has no forgiveness and no commitment. "Move on" seems to be the way couples are approaching their marriages more and more lately. It's all about me—the *wow-now*. Check out the television programs and see how men and women are being portrayed. Some women are doing the very things they have criticized men for in the past.

HUSBANDS AND WIVES:

What kind of Legacy do we want to leave our children? We rationalize and deny—compromising integrity and values for our children. We're lowering the bar and creating new norms. My parents used to say, that just because others do it, doesn't make it right. So why would we follow the herd?

It's true, *Commitment precedes Investment.* We know what's right and wrong. Yet harmful vices are becoming more and more common. Porn is up, drinking is up, drugs are up, divorce is up, suicides of young people are up, theft and corruption are up, world debt and greed are up. Couples don't get married. Why would they, when there's a back door and they can love'em and leave'em? Selfishness leads to more selfishness. Chasing the *me* race—the wow-now of instant gratification—only leads to more emptiness. It's never enough!

A woman's loyalty is tested when her man has nothing.
A man's loyalty is tested when he has everything.

"When we choose not to focus on what is missing from our lives but are grateful for the abundance that's present…we experience heaven on earth."

— Sarah Breathnach

Why does it take major world tragedies such as Haiti, New Orleans, Fort McMurray, High River, and Japan's nuclear disaster, to pour out our hearts? But in our own marriage and family we will abandon them like a rusted old pick up truck instead of responding with loving kindness.

We can choose how to approach our marriage and relationships through *unity* or *control*. Control is dividing, not uniting.

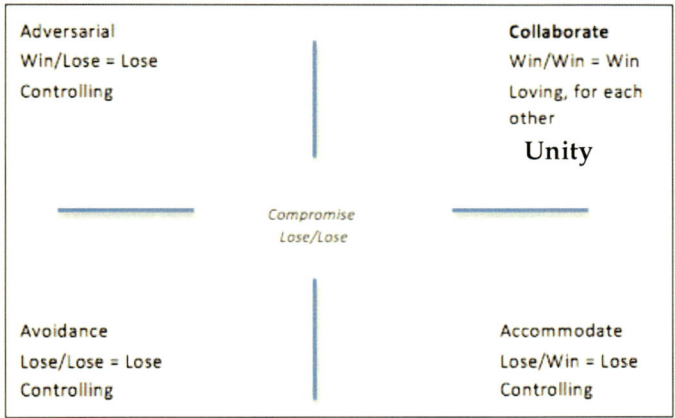

Adversarial Win/Lose = Lose Controlling		**Collaborate** Win/Win = Win Loving, for each other **Unity**
	Compromise Lose/Lose	
Avoidance Lose/Lose = Lose Controlling		Accommodate Lose/Win = Lose Controlling

Collaborate   We are ... "For Each Other"

In marriage, husband and wife are a team of unity.

I'm for you no matter what. We might disagree, but we care more about each other and our relationship than the topic or who's right. We forgive each other no matter what. We are respectful and honest. We make a promise to each other and are committed to each other.

UNITY:

U   **Uplift** each other: Encouraging, patient, kind and a desire to understand not criticize or blame.

N   **Needs.** We meet each other's needs by learning about them, asking them, and putting their needs ahead of our wants or insecurities.

I   **Intimacy** (In-to-me-see). Having the courage, trust, and willingness to be vulnerable with a heart of gratitude.

T   **Trust.** By living to our word. Giving each other a safe place to communicate.

Y   **Yield.** To one another. We put our partners needs ahead of our wants. We recognize and appreciate their strengths that complement ours.

It takes a giving heart to have a fulfilling marriage. When you and your spouse are having problems, remember to stop and work at understanding your spouse's perspective. Be patient with each other—the gift is in the giving.

CHAPTER NINE

CHARACTER

Grandpa said to his grandson one day, "Son, life's about two words."

His grandson asked, "What's that, Grandpa?"

"Good decisions," Grandpa replied with a nod.

"How do you make good decisions, Grandpa?" the boy asked, his eyes waiting in wonderment.

"Oh," Grandpa paused, "that's about one word."

Again, his grandson asked, "What's that?" He waited curiously for more.

"Wisdom," Grandpa softly replied.

"How do I get wisdom, Grandpa?"

With no expression, Grandpa said, "That's about two words, son."

Patiently, he asked, "Two more words? What are those?"

Grandpa's eyes were strong and soft as he gave his grandson a little smile and said, "Bad Decisions."

Do good decisions come from good character, or does good character come from good decisions? Good character helps us to make good choices. Good character doesn't just happen. Good choices are made from knowing what is right and wrong and wanting to make the right choices. Wanting to make the right choice comes from a heart and mind that loves God and loves others, as well ourselves. *I can take time to do it right or take time to do it over.*

I've been pretty thick-headed, stubborn, and somewhat blind at times during my life. It's taken many painful trials to put 2+2 together. Character is developed and revealed by the tests in our life. Life is a gift but life is also a test to see if we will cherish and honour who and what we have been given.

Character is more than wisdom. Yet having wisdom helps build good character. Being responsible and accountable is good character. Having compassion, understanding, and forgiveness is good character. Seeing the good, encouraging the good, and doing good, is good character. Being patient, kind, and persevering is good character. Trusting our Father in Heaven is good character.

What we focus on, what we're taught, what we choose, what we say, what we believe, what we value, what we do, and how we treat each other—all reveal our character.

Little things are big. We know the saying: "If you can't be trusted with little then you can't be trusted with much." Most women will confirm that it's the little things that count the most. I let men know it's about simple acts of kindness and integrity. Trust is earned in a spirit of kindness with truth. It takes vulnerability, commitment, and the will to stay on track—one step at a time. When we tell a lie or don't do the right thing with our spouse, with our children, at work or with our friends, we're damaging our character. We're hurting ourselves and, more importantly, we're hurting others.

So why do we overlook the little things? Do you say what you mean and mean what you say? Is your word good? Sometimes we have good intentions, but we don't deliver. Some are more reliable and committed, but we all fall short. We break our promise. *My word needs to be more important than my want.*

My words proclaim me, my actions convict me.

My lack of integrity has hurt others and myself. I've stolen, I've smoked drugs, I've fallen to porn, I've had sex outside marriage. I've wronged my employers. I've used people. I've dishonoured the one I love, causing her to lose trust in me. I've lied and betrayed. I've let fear discourage me and control my emotions. I've escaped and let depression control my mind. It's true the enemy wants to steal, kill, and destroy our lives and our relationships. *When we cheat we hide.*

The selfish and unhealthy things I've done have caused a lot of hurt to myself and to those close to me. Escaping to wrong choices affected my marriage, which in turn hurt my children. My career and financial welfare also suffered because of poor choices. Until I started to look at my life, through God's eyes, I wouldn't have been able to start to make the healthy loving changes needed for me to grow. A few years ago, I wrote: *there's joy in discipline.* I was puzzled as to why I wrote this. Then I realized, it's because there ain't no joy in un-discipline! So now I remind myself that it's the benefits of being disciplined that I enjoy.

Fortunately, the mistakes and failures I've made don't define me. They don't have to define you, either. Just because I fail doesn't mean I'm a failure. As Zig Ziglar says, "God don't sponsor flops." *Sometimes we win and sometimes we learn.*

I may sound like I'm preaching, but I'm actually talking to myself. I've a long way to go, but being aware of where I need to grow helps me take steps in the right direction. I've also learned not to beat myself up or live in guilt and condemnation. God has forgiven me and will be there to forgive me again—and, I know I want to give my heart to Him and do what is right and loving.

Practicing good character also helps break toxic habits or addictions. If I was to ask, do you have any addictions, and you said no, then I would ask you to rethink your answer. We all have addictions. Some may want to call them bad habits, escapes, or vices but they are ultimately addictions. Serge LeClerc said, "People don't have addictions to feel good, they have addictions to stop feeling bad." Addictions are rooted in fear and habitual thinking, heavily focused on selfishness. Addictions hang on because of our denial, unwillingness to change, and undisciplined thinking to control that which is controlling us. Admitting our addictions takes courage. Taking action requires more courage. Good character takes courage (and some help from those who can truly help and support).

Common addictions in our society include smoking, drinking, gambling, porn, drugs, and overeating. But, what about some others that are less talked about? These may include running from relationship to relationship, resenting, manipulating and using people, masturbating, texting, social media, spending, shopping, internet surfing, emailing, talking, not talking, worrying, blaming, criticising, arguing, complaining, gossiping, hiding, avoiding, enabling, controlling, attacking, abusing, rejecting, boasting, interrupting, fighting, depression, needing to be right, appearance and vanity, power, status, significance, security, seeking attention, rudeness, anger, pity-me victim mentalities, stubborn pride, negativity, and self-centeredness. Okay, what's left? If I don't respect myself and love myself—if I don't believe that I am made by a loving God and made in His image—then how am I going to be encouraged to stop believing the lies, or stop the toxic thinking and addictions? I can keep on thinking that I'm not good enough and try to cover it up like so many of us do, or I can start to love who I am and build the character of value that I was made with from the beginning.

I made it about me.

Many of us don't feel overly good about ourselves. We tend to live in one of three places: I'm not good enough, I'm not as bad as the other person, and I'm better than the other person. What I think of myself, what I think others think about me, and how I view others is one of my biggest struggles.

Thoughts and feelings like these depend on how we are raised, our personality, and our beliefs. You don't have to look too far to see the *selfish*-thinking in our lives and world: marriages, dating relationships, workplace relationships, family, sporting community, schools, government, and our country. It's in our *minds* and *hearts* much of the time. I've noticed about myself, that when I put someone down, it actually is a way of trying to put myself up. I don't want to think badly of myself or be thought of in a negative way, so I either view the other person in a critical way or try to make myself look good. I turn to either critical thinking or boastful pride.

Neither of these ways are good. It does hurtful things to me and it damages the possibility of having a good relationship with those close to me or those I know. Often these thoughts come from feeling rejected, unwanted or unvalued by someone important to me. This is a dangerous place for my mind to go. So what's the antidote? How do we get past the negative, self-centered, insecure, and judgmental thinking?

It boils down to: *do I want to give love, or do I want to be loved?* My attitude, my character, and my thinking are all rooted in one of these two. It's really that simple and true.

Wanting *to be loved* instead of wanting *to love* can create emptiness inside (by design). Much of our worldview says, "I just want *to be* happy." Chasing this race never ends. Am I willing to be honest and go through the pain of change? It takes time and desire to make it right. I didn't get messy overnight, and I can't get cleaned up overnight either.

And then the day came
when the risk to remain tight in a bud
was more painful than the risk
it took to blossom.
Anaïs Nin

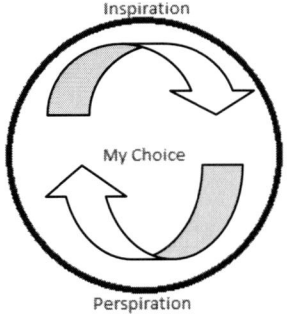

In the book *The Purpose Driven Life*, Rick Warren writes, "The way you see yourself shapes your life."

> *"We don't see things as they are,*
> *we see things as we are."*
> – Anaïs Nin

I needed to write out how I saw my life and myself in order to better understand how I could improve my character. Ask yourself some important questions, such as these.

I am _____.

I see my way in life as, _____.

My mind is powerful and my heart is important. I need to take the time to reflect on thinking and doing the right things in the right way. I want to be mature, of integrity, with purpose, and kind. I want to grow personally, help others, and use the gifts I've been given. I also know that worry, anxiety, and insecurity can cause me to get discouraged or depressed, which doesn't allow me to solve problems, be thankful, or help others.

It's no secret that stinking thinking, or positive loving thoughts make a difference to our wellbeing. There are lots of books and speakers that share how important it is to motivate our hearts and minds.

The challenge is realizing our motive. Remember, we are more filled up when we are giving—the gift is in the giving. So meditating or reflecting, daily or hourly, helps our mind, our heart, and our relationships. It's wise for us to have verses and quotes that we can read or recall, to keep us pointed and motivated in the right direction.

"Finally, my brothers and sisters, always think about what is true. Think about what is noble, right and pure. Think about what is lovely and worthy of respect. If anything is excellent or worthy of praise, think about those kinds of things."

– Philippians 4:8

Ultimately, our character is based on our motive—our heart. Good character *is* loving. When they asked what was the greatest commandment, *"Jesus replied, Love the Lord your God with all your heart and with all your soul and with all your mind. This is the first and greatest commandment. And the second is like it: Love your neighbor as yourself. All the Law and the Prophets hang on these two commandments." Matthew 22: 37- 40*

How we treat one another stems from our character—our heart. Don't believe the lies that you are not worthy, and don't put anyone down out of desire for revenge or to make them feel unworthy. We are all made in God's image. None of us are better than each other.

When I realize our Father in Heaven loves me, and when I hold on to that each day and each hour, I can let go of my insecurity of wanting *to be loved*. Instead of making it about me, I can follow Jesus who loved his Father and each one of us. I can lay down my life and sacrifice my selfish wants for the welfare of another. That's what good character is really about. Growing good character will enrich your relationships.

CHAPTER TEN

FORGIVENESS

Forgiveness is a choice.

When there is forgiveness in one's heart, there is healing.

Love is committed,
It does not quit.
Love is courageous,
It does not hide.
Love faces fear,
And always perseveres.
Love trusts God,
When hope seems gone.
Love takes courage,
to forgive and keep on.

This book is meant to help motivate men and women to love one another—deep in our hearts. Likely one of the most important qualities in loving someone is forgiveness. Ruth Graham says that marriage takes two good forgivers.

Not one of us has gone through life without being betrayed or betraying someone else. Especially the ones we are closest to. Some of us keep choosing patterns that cause us to repeat the hurts. When I ask God to help me forgive, He shows me how He forgave all my wrongs. We are all selfish, lost, and we don't always realize what we do.

It's not right or loving to repay wrong with wrong. Truth can be spoken with kindness. When you love someone, you forgive and hang in there with them even when they fail you. Forgiveness trumps justice. The way to deal with those who betray and hurt you is to forgive them.

Forgiveness will shine the love needed to repair the hurt and restore one's heart. Resentment hurts you more than it does the one you resent. Those who've hurt you cannot hurt you anymore, unless you hang on to the pain and keep resenting them. Resentment and revenge looks back and focuses on the past. Love looks forward and focuses on the future. See the pain as a gift of learning and that forgiveness is healing.

Another way that helps me forgive is to see the hurt I have caused. So how could I not extend the forgiveness I'd want extended to me, even if the one I love doesn't? Being accountable for my thinking and behaviour is important and really helps me to forgive.

Forgiveness is not easy, it's not fair and it requires much sacrifice. *It realizes the other person needs my forgiveness more than I need fair treatment.* It also says I'm not the fixer of someone else. God has an amazing way of reaching someone at the end of their rope with redeeming grace.

I'm learning to stop asking the *whys* in life. Why did this happen to me? Why did that person do that? Why didn't my parents raise me different? Why did God let that happen? This is self-centered victim thinking.

Even though I don't like the hurt that has happened, I'm thankful for the insight and passion it gave me to help men and women in their marriages and their personal lives. God has an amazing way of turning the mess into a message.

Everyone is fighting a battle you know nothing about. Be kind, always. We all want hope. And in some way, we all face a fear of losing hope. Whether it's in our marriage, our health, our career, or our finances. We all want to know everything is going to be okay. This is why us humans try to control. Our trust and faith seem to go out the window. But who is our faith in? Others? Ourselves? Ultimately, our faith needs to be in God. God is our Creator and our everlasting loving Father.

When I withhold forgiveness, it's a form of control. I'm wanting to repay the hurt. I'm holding on to resentment or blame. In my hurt I don't want to feel bad about myself or to think that I am in the wrong, thus I overlook my wrongs. Not forgiving and holding on to resentment can be a disguised feeling of superiority.

I can sometimes think I'm better than the other person, or that they are the problem. This has no compassion for what the other person is going through or has gone through in their life. Secondly, it's very hypocritical and voids responsibility for my selfish behaviours.

If I practice un-forgiveness (resentment, revenge, blame) then it will become habitual thinking and behaviour. If I practice forgiveness then it too can become habitual, which is for my benefit. If I'm to become more loving, which forgiveness is a very significant part, then how am I going to get my heart there unless I have something/someone to forgive. Like anything, I'm not going to get good or improve if I don't practice thinking and doing it. My golf swing, my writing, my finances, my vocation, or my relationships only have good results when I practice the good things in good ways.

My grandad gave me a big hug one day outside their high-rise condo in Burnaby, British Columbia. I was about 33 years old. My kids were about 10, 8 and 3 at the time and were inside with my grandma. He must have known something about my struggles, or just felt he had to tell me this. He said, "Son, marriage is about commitment." I didn't reply out loud, but I thought to myself, "No, it's about love." Little did I realize, at that time, that love *is* about commitment.

Human beings are designed for committed love, not conditional love. Forgiveness is a committed love (unconditional). Here's proof. If a parent was to make their love conditional for their child, how do you think that child would feel? Likely, they'd feel they couldn't meet the mark to earn their parent's love. If God's love was conditional, there's no way He would've sacrificed His Son Jesus for our sins and our lives. We couldn't have met the mark. Forgiveness goes hand-in-hand with commitment. Even though parents discipline their child, to correct, their love isn't conditional and their love forgives.

Conditional love is not love. Conditional means self-seeking – *I'll love my husband if*, or *I'll love my wife when*. Love holds no record of wrongs – love forgives.

A world of Un-Forgiveness is a brutal and ugly alternative.

Our world needs forgiveness in our marriages, families, workplaces, communities, and countries. Let's give everything we have to let someone know they are worth it—because God knows we are *all* worth it!

Knowing Man's greatest need and Woman's greatest need, for Significance and Security plus the retreating and attacking/rejecting, can help us see that forgiving, instead of automatically fighting or flighting, will help build-up our love versus breakdown our marriage. To love your spouse with forgiveness and understanding is to love in the way God intended. Forgiveness is probably the biggest transformation we will go through in our lives. It is likely the most significant ingredient in the recipe of love. Faith, Hope, and Love … and the Greatest of these is Love.

God's love for us was given at the time He created us (in His image) and then after we fell to sin (separating ourselves from Him). He promised to send His Son to forgive us and restore us back to Him. God is sinless, pure and eternally loving. Yes He disciplines (as a loving Father does), for correction, but He also paid the price and sacrificed His only Son's life, Jesus Christ.

His way is loving, and when our relationships are hurting He asks, and hopes (giving us choice) that we will make amends by forgiving and re-uniting. He forgave us, and took accountability for us. He knew we were vulnerable, yet gave us choice to follow Him and to love Him. When we were tempted, we made the mistake and fell to temptation. But our Father always forgives and hopes we will turn to Him and give our heart to loving one another.

If I could give you a gift, it would be to love through the hurt, so your spouse knows how important they are to you.

You are who you are for a reason.

You are part of an intricate plan.

You're a precious and unique design,

Called God's special woman or man.

You look like you look for a reason.

Our God made no mistake.

He knit you together within the womb.

You're just what he wanted to make.

The parents you had were the ones he chose.

And no matter how you may feel,

They were custom-designed with God's plan in mind.

And they bear the Master's seal.

No, that trauma you faced was not easy.

And God wept that it hurt you so,

But it was allowed to shape your heart,

So that into his likeness you'd grow.

You are who you are for a reason.

You've been formed by the Master's rod.

You are who you are, beloved,

Because there is a God.

— Russell Kelfer

CHAPTER ELEVEN

IN CLOSING

I hope what I have shared has given you insight and inspiration that will help your marriage, your relationships, and your life. I hope you will know that you are an amazing and very special person—God made you and He loves you.

I hope that knowing Man's greatest need (Significance) and Woman's greatest need (Security) plus the Single Biggest Reason Why Marriage Breaks Down (Retreating and Rejecting/Attacking out of fear) and how to build them up, will give you some renewed ways of thinking, behaving, and a change of heart. Because we can be selfish and struggle with our fears and emotions, our relationships can be challenging.

Yet we can know these trials also help us to persevere, increase our trust in God, and love more deeply—becoming the person He calls us to be. Your habits, your understanding, your communication, and your motive—to give or to get—will greatly affect your marriage, your family, and your relationships.

UCG – Knowing thyself and learning about the ones close to you is important, and then having the heart and will to put your love into daily action is how the gift of love fills our lives.

It's not greener on the other side of the fence, it's greener where you water it.

Instead of being blind, we can understand. Instead of letting our unhealthy habits control our thoughts, we can retrain our brain. Instead of being selfish and stubborn with pride and ego, we can give, forgive, and experience love.

Love is a choice. Love, choice, and believing are the three greatest gifts we've been given. They go hand-in-hand. God gives us His love and has created us to love, to choose, and to believe in His love.

Ultimately, He is our greatest need, as God is love. He loves each and every one of us. Thank you for reading my book and I hope the next chapter, *My Journey*, helps you.

CHAPTER TWELVE

MY JOURNEY

My Granddad said at my wedding that my wife may sometimes need a 2 x 4 to get through to me. Ignorance is bliss, but it still hurts. Maybe I'm stubborn, naïve, or just a sucker for love. If I had the crystal ball on my wedding day and had seen how my marriage would turn out, I wouldn't have believed it. But Granddad was right. I'm not sure what happened, but I went from a four-year-old exploring the world on my bike (okay, exploring my neighbor hood) to a fat kid who got teased and bullied.

I don't think my Grandma Taylor would mind if I blamed her for my sweet tooth. Mom and Dad would ship me out for the summer to my Grandma and Granddad's in the Okanagan. I had it pretty good. The lake, two boys next door with horses, all the kids at the campground across the lane to play with, and a big games room with a ping-pong table. I pretty much lived in my bathing suit and got to go boating and waterskiing often. The summers were good for about the next seven or eight years. My grandma was awesome! Every night before bed, we played chinese-checkers or rummy, with a bowl of cereal and brown sugar. Granddad mostly taught me manners. He pretty much worked alone in his wood shop most of the time.

I'd help Grandma in their big garden but I think I ate more peas, raspberries, and cherries than I put in the pail. I was pretty chunky by grade one (thanks, Grandma) and younger than most in my class at the age of five.

Mom had to go back to work when my brother and sister were little, to help pay the bills. So they went to the babysitter's while I was on my own over lunch and after school. I'd watch TV and eat what Mom prepared the night before. I now see why it's good for moms to be home with their kids when they are young. Before the end of grade one I started to get teased and bullied—it continued throughout elementary. Even though I was chunky, I loved hockey. I'd play shinney all day at the outdoor rink across the street. But being overweight made it tough to keep up or get the puck. I started to play league by grade three but quit a few years later as I didn't think I was good enough. It wasn't fun anymore.

My family moved quite a bit and I was in and out of schools. Making new friends wasn't easy. From grade six to grade ten I went to six different schools.

Being fat, insecure, and sensitive really sucks when you're thirteen and your buds are gettin' the girls. It also didn't help that my dad had playboy and penthouse magazines laying around the house. Unhealthy habits became an escape.

We moved half way through grade ten, from Regina to Edmonton. I went to the largest high school in the city—it had a pretty bad reputation for drugs. My younger brother was dying of muscle cancer so we had to move for chemo treatments. Mom had to quit work to look after my brother, and my parents lost a lot of money moving back to Alberta—it was a tough time. I grew about six inches in grade ten, and girls were becoming a possibility (a long shot, but still!). It was tough fitting in half way through grade ten, but I had some Mormon friends that bridged the gap (except for the name calling that happens in high school). I managed to squeek by with mediocore grades and had hopes of getting my first car. Dad promised he'd pay half—look out, Chevy 350 ss Nova, here I come. One day he surprised me, and there it was in front of our west-end condo—a beautiful four-door, faded-yellow 318, three-on-the-tree Dodge Dart, that only cost $400 dollars. Girls' heads are gonna turn...the other way.

During the summer before grade eleven, I was fifteen years old and had no driver's license. I had to go see this girl I really liked, but wasn't sixteen for another six months. Busted—2x4 time. Dad graced me with a thirty-day sentence (and called the cops—or least he told me he did to set me straight).

In grade eleven and the following summer my four-door faded-yellow Dodge Dart allowed me to skip class, go to house parties, smoke some dope, and yes, get some girls. Can't believe my parents didn't find out. Failing math (my best subject) tells you where I was headed. I remember driving to the Mormon church for

Saturday night dances with my not-so-Mormon buds. The girls were pretty and flirted lots. Grade eleven was a slippery slope. By grade twelve, I had to wake up and make a choice: keep going or make new friends.

I was eighteen when my girlfriend (soon to be bride) moved to Calgary with her family—her dad was transferred. We listened to her dad and got married instead of living together. We were nineteen and going to live happily ever after. By age 23, we bought our first house and started a family. I was starting to grow up (so I thought). With three children, working full time in the oil patch and fifteen years of night classes, time flew by. As the family grew, our marriage grew apart. Even though we did our best to raise our children, the fighting, selfishness, bad habits, and my addictions got worse. It's amazing how much my childhood and teen years played into my poor choices and insecurities as an adult. I wanted my kids to have it better and to do better than I did. I didn't want them to be teased. I wanted them to be good in sports and school (like most parents, right?). We put all three in swim club and the boys in hockey for ten to fifteen years. I coached and we volunteered in many of the kids' activities. Helping in their school while on shift work, reading, playing, and family campouts were things we did lots as a family.

I really wanted to be engaged in my children's lives and development, so they would know they were important and have lots of self-confidence.

Yet from the wedding night and throughout my marriage, I felt rejected. This caused me to escape to the wrong things (porn, adultery, alcohol, you get the picture). Trying to control the pain with the very thing that caused the pain—stemming from my childhood and youth. Why does it take a lifetime? Why so many 2x4s?

I've jumped from relationship to relationship since my divorce. Even before I divorced, I jumped into whatever I thought was going to make me happy. I traded *the sliver of pleasure for the mountain of pain.*

I raised 20 million dollars and started a new manufacturing company as we separated towards divorce. I wanted to be successful so I could find that special someone to love me.

I shared the dream of a new manufacturing plant with prospective employees and investors. Hired 130 employees in a year and a half. Created a work culture where they felt good about who they were. I wanted them to know they weren't just a number and they were more important than the products or mistakes we made.

I hadn't been a CEO or entrepreneur before, but I read the book *Rich Dad Poor Dad* and believed I had the business acumen and passion to make it happen. We did 22 million dollars in revenue the year I left. It was bought by a very large company and is still going today, with a capacity to out-produce its competitors and do 100 million dollars per year in revenue. One of my management team introduced me to a colors personality book. I hired all my staff using this tool. People would always say to me, "How do you know me so well?" I wanted us to understand each other and I wanted to be able to connect with and motivate people in a way they needed.

Then—BOOM! It all fell apart. I lost it all! My family, my business, and most importantly, I lost my belief in who I was. Maybe I didn't know who I was. Unfortunately, many of us are not *awoken* until we're *broken*. It seems we don't want to look at how selfish we are until we've hit bottom, lost a loved one, or lost everything we have. I'm here to share with you that you don't have to ride the elevator to the bottom, nor do you have to stay in self-pity and blame mode.

On September 17, 2008, my life changed direction.

I had a haircut appointment for 10:00 am and an 11:00 am meeting with a pastor at a local church in Lethbridge, Alberta. For about 8 months it had been building inside me to move out on this woman I was living with. I knew it was wrong, and I didn't want to hurt her. I was still married (separated) but living with someone else. Finally, the pressure got so strong that I called the church where my friends attended. I needed to find out what to do. My life was a wreck and I was at the bottom with no hope and no rope.

I realized the ten o'clock hair appointment and eleven o'clock pastor appointment were too close together (my low Gold of not being organized was apparent). I called and rescheduled my haircut for 9:00 am. When I finished my haircut, the church called to reschedule for 2:00 pm. This was no coincidence—this was divine intervention. I had four hours to wait, and nothing to do. I was a total wreck! My grandparents had given me a bible. I was not a church-goer. I was not a bible thumper.

I hated reading, and the bible would have been the last book I'd pick up to read. I knew a verse or two and, as a teenager, my family went to church for a while after my 12-year-old brother died of cancer. I remember, when I was 5 or 6, singing *Jesus Loves Me this I know, for the Bible Tells Me So.*

In 1982, I was married in a church and the vows exchanged were from the "love chapter" (1ˢᵗ Corinthians 13: 4-8), not that I really knew what it was all about.

On September 17, 2008, I sat by myself at the table and read the whole book of John out loud. Rereading many versus over and over, eating up every word that Jesus spoke. I couldn't not believe. I just kept pouring my amazement into the Word. After 2 ½ to 3 hours, I closed my bible from back to front and said, "This is the Book of Love, God is Love." I knew!

I went to my two o'clock appointment and saw the pastor. I told him I didn't need to see him. I told him that I just read the book of John. But I told him my life story anyways. He said he would've recommended the book of John and that I needed to read it two more times in the next week. So I did.

On September 17ᵗʰ, I knew God was love, and I knew Jesus. Something amazing happened inside me. I felt complete peace, it was like I was floating and all I could see is this golden light as I could barley keep my eyes open. This feeling was going through my whole being, even as I drove to Edmonton and to Fort McMurray for some work I was doing. I could barely keep my eyes open, just little slits, and this feeling of floating and golden light kept going inside me. All I could say was, "Let them know You, just love them, let them know You." I knew why He sent His Son Jesus (God's Spirit in Flesh).

God came in Jesus Christ to save us from our sins, just like he promised when Adam and Eve fell to temptation and chose to separate themselves from God. He didn't send His Son to condemn us, but to forgive us and save us (John 3:16). To know Him and to believe who He is, to know how much He loves each and every one of us, is the greatest gift of all.

I thought my life would get better automatically after this. Like flicking on a light switch, I thought everything was going to instantly get better. Little did I realize much change was needed. The battle of my mind began. My thinking, my behaviours of insecurity, and my irresponsible decisions needed a major overhaul. I didn't realize how much I needed to grow. I didn't realize how much I needed God's love, God's way, and God's truth to keep me on the right path.

Even my brief second marriage was a choice of selfishness, not of following what was right and loving. I've had to look at my motives, my thinking, and my patterns since then. I have fallen away many times, yet each time the 2x4 hits I get a reminder to repoint my heart to God. I've studied and learned about emotional abuse, over-dependency, addictions, controlling ways, love languages, upbringing, gender, personalities, values, and beliefs. Most of all, I am learning what love is and to follow God's loving way. I'm thankful for the trials and the teachings. And there are many people I need to thank. And for those I've hurt, I wish had done it differently.

I had to choose: persevere or quit. Fight, flight, or forgive. My son sent a quote a few years back when he saw what I was going through. It said, "It's not how hard you get kicked, it's how hard you can get kicked and get back up again." God tells us hundreds of times in His word, "Fear not, I am with you." The reality is we're not meant to do it alone. With God, all things are possible.

I encourage you to read the book of John and the other three gospels. I urge you to read about the many characters in God's word. Abraham and Joseph in the book of Genesis, Moses in the book of Exodus, Jacob, David and how he came to fight Goliath, Ruth, Ester, Jeremiah, Hosea—read everything you can about His redeeming love. Also the New Testament Covenant of Jesus Christ: The book of John, Matthew, Mark, and Luke where Jesus came to give us life and the truth to God's love and our journey with Him. Read how God changed Saul to apostle Paul and how He sacrificed his life and his heart to bring the good news of Jesus Christ to all.

Read about Peter, John, James, and more. Read the book of Revelation of Jesus Christ, where he says, "Look, I am coming soon! Blessed is the one who keeps the words of the prophecy written in this scroll."

My journey hasn't ended and God will finish the good work He started in me, in time. Everyone's story is important. God's truth and promises are lifegiving:

"being confident of this, that he who began a good work in you will carry it on to completion until the day of Christ Jesus." Philippians 1:6

"For God so loved the world that He gave His one and only Son, that who ever believes in him shall not perish but have eternal life. For God did not send His Son into the world to condemn the world, but to save the world through him." John 3: 16-17

My life changed the day I read the book of John—it was the most amazing time of my life. Complete peace in the midst of wreckage—amazing grace! It hasn't been easy. I still battle the escapes, the instant pleasures, the resentments, and the stubborn pity parties. Rejection has been a struggle my whole life. Looking for love in all the wrong places. Loneliness and brokeness can cause us to do some desperate things. Little did I know then that I was running away from my own fear. When I knew God loved me and looked in the mirror, I could stop believing the lies and start believing the truth.

I believe a woman is attracted to a man that knows God, trusts God, and follows Jesus with all his heart, mind, and soul. I didn't know this before. I am thankful for His calling and His Grace every day.

The Cross is *Vertical* and *Horizontal*.
Jesus put his *Faith* only in God, vertically upward. Jesus gave forgiveness for all, horizontally outward.

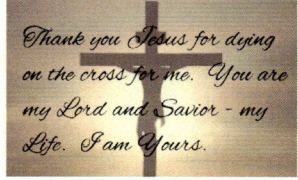

Faith in God, *Forgiveness* to all.

He finished the work His Father set out to do. God loves us. He made us and He wants us to be with Him for eternity. That is why he delivered on His promise in the garden, from the time we fell to temptation and separated from Him. He said He would send His Son Jesus. As soon as we sinned He forgave us. This is why Jesus came to us—to save us from our sins and to restore us and reunite us to Him. He paid the price in full with His love, His Son's life, so that we may have eternal life with Him. I invite you to accept His free gift of love and grace. My prayers are with you, In Jesus' name.

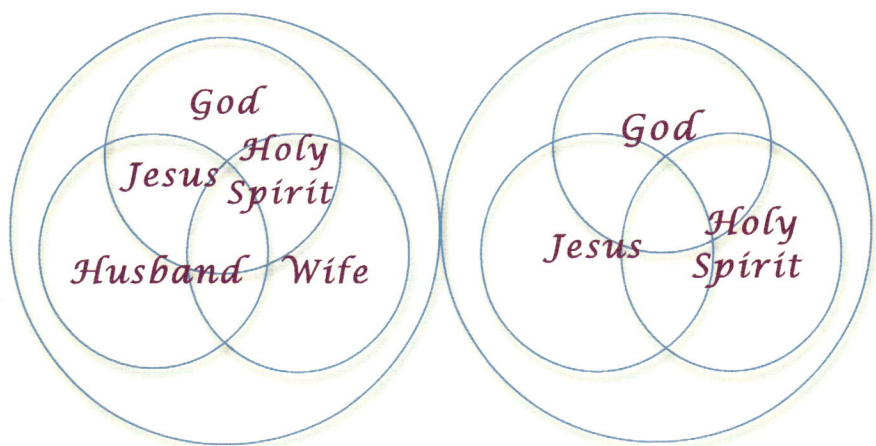

Let Us make mankind in Our image. Who is Us, and who is Our? God, Jesus, Holy Spirit - Distinctly Individual & All in One. This is how important Husband and Wife are.

I like to share, that when God made man He said it was *good*. And when He made woman He said, *wooooman !!!* ☺

When God said, It is not good for the man to be alone. I will make him a helper suitable for him , He wasn't just talking about a two by four holder.

He gave man the greatest gift He could give him as a mate. *The man said, "Her bones have come from my bones. Her body has come from my body. She will be named 'woman,' because she was taken out of a man." - Genesis 2: 23*

177

Woman was made from man and for man, not from his feet or his head, to be beneath or above, but from his side, to walk along side, under his arm to be protected and near his heart to be loved. Where he is weak she is strong, where she is weak he is strong. Husband and Wife are completers not competers. They are the greatest team between two human beings. When God is at the top and the center of their lives they will know what His love is all about and how to love one another.

I say to men, remember … God gave you woman, a beautiful gift made in His image, to cherish and to honor with all your heart, might, and will. By putting God's heart and will first, with all your heart, you will be better able to love your wife, your family, your community and the people in our world.

Even though my passion to help Husbands and Wives gain insight to what I believe is the greatest need of man and woman, plus the breakdown, I also wanted to share God's revealing love. Without our Father and our Lord and Saviour Jesus Christ, we would not be here or have the choice for eternity in heaven. Our hope and faith is in Him. Thank you, Father, in Jesus' name. Amen.

Loving through the hurt—suffering is not painful when I want to sacrafice myself for the welfare of another so that they will know God's amazing love. God bless you and thank you for reading this book.

Dedication

I dedicate this book to my Father in Heaven and to the ones I love. For without God I would not be writing this book or have the love in my heart to give. I also dedicate this book to my children—Jessica, Jonathan, and Jordan, they mean the world to me; they are so very special—thank you for being the best kids I could ever ask for! I love you! Oh, and I have an amazing grandson named Gunnar and number two on the way! Thank you, Rob and Jessica. And another *oh,* to my son Jon and his new bride Sarah, congrats! To my mom and dad, my brother and sister, I am so grateful—life wasn't easy but there was much love in our family. Thanks, Dad and Mom, for everything you have done. I want to give a special thank you to God for my Mom, she has been there for me through all the trials and the growth—thank you, Mom! You are a gift from God. And, to my close friends who kept praying for me (prayer works!). I pray we will *all* be together in heaven one day.

And last but not least, I thank all the men, women,

and couples I have shared my story and insight with—and you who are reading this now. Thank you with all my heart! God bless you.

About the Author

Brent was born in Calgary, Alberta, Canada, in 1962. He is the oldest of three children, one of which passed away with cancer at age twelve when Brent was 15 years old. Brent was married at the age of 19 and a few years later was a father to Jessica, his oldest, and his two sons, Jonathan and Jordan. They travelled from town to town throughout Alberta to the arenas and swimming pools for games and competitions. He coached hockey and worked in the oil patch for many years. One of his highlights was pioneering a new manufacturing company, which he lost and was one of the straws that broke the camel's back, so to speak.

Many trials came his way. From broken to awoken—he knew he wanted to write a book to help couples. He embarked on a journey to discover Hiz & Herz Greatest Need and what breaks up the marriage. He pursued several certifications, researched and read many books on men and women, personalities, and the family. Gaining more insight and passion, he surveyed and shared his discovery with thousands of men and women.

Brent Taylor is a speaker and relationship coach for couples and individuals.

He is the owner of C4 Insight and specializes in personality profiling, marriage coaching, leadership coaching, and team building.

After many years in business his passion moved him towards a deeper calling and training. From: True Colors, Emergenetics, Disc, Brian Tracey (Focal Point) business coaching, significant research on men, women, and family – to personal training sessions for marriage, relationships and personal growth. Most importantly, he gives primary credit for his true growth and passion to God, who has grown him to the true calling of his heart. Helping others from the heart.

Brent is a keynote speaker and coach, who shares his story and inspires men and women in their marriage, their family, and in their personal lives.

To contact Brent and learn more about his book and programs, or to arrange speaking events and workshops, please visit: **hizandherz.ca**

References and Recommended Reading

Banschick, M. (2016). The Intelligent Divorce: The High Failure Rate of Second and Third Marriages. *Psychology Today*. www.psychologytoday.com/blog/the-intelligent-divorce/201202/the-high-failure-rate-second-and-third-marriages

Chapman, G. (1992). *The Five Love Languages: The Secret to Love That Lasts*. Northfield Publishing: Chicago, IL, USA. ISBN-13: 978-0-8024-1270-6

Crowe, C. (1996). *Jerry Maguire* (Film). TriStar Pictures. Gracie Films: USA.

Dictionary.com (2016). Definition: *Patience*. Retrieved: October 16, 2016, at http://www.dictionary.com/browse/patience

Eaker Weil, B. (1999). *Make Up, Don't Break Up: Finding and Keeping Love for Singles and Couples*. Adams Media: Avon, MA, USA. ISBN-13:978-1605503608

Ethridge, S., & Arterburn, S. (2009). *Every Woman's Battle: Discovering God's Plan for Sexual and Emotional Fulfillment*. WaterBrook Press: Colorado Springs, CO, USA. ISBN-13: 978-0307457981

Farrar, S., & Branon, D. (1996). *Point Man: How a Man Can Lead His Family*. Multnomah Books, Men's Leadership Ministries: Frisco, TX, USA. ISBN-13: 978-1-59052-126-7

Farrel, B., & Farrel, P. (2007). *Men Are Waffles and Women Are Spaghetti: Understanding and Delighting in Your Differences*. Harvest House Publishers: Eugene, OR, USA. ISBN-13: 978-0-7369-1961-6

Gray, J. (1992). *Men are from Mars and Women are from Venus: The Classic Guide to Understanding the Opposite Sex*. HarperCollins Publishers Inc.: New York, NY, USA. ISBN-13: 978-0-06-057421-5

Gungor, M. (2008). *Laugh Your Way to a Better Marriage: Unlocking the Secrets to Life, Love, and Marriage*. Laugh Your Way America LLC, Atria Paperback, Simon & Schuster: New York, NY, USA. ISBN-13: 978-1-4165-3605-5

Gungor, M. (2011). *Men Matter: The Importance of Fathers*. The Mark Gungor Show. http://www.markgungorshow.com/show/8220

Gurian, M., Stevens, K., Henley, P., & Trueman, T. (2011). *Boys and Girls Learn Differently: A Guide for Teachers and Parents*, Revised 10th Anniversary Edition. Jossey-Bass, A Wiley Imprint: San Francisco, CA, USA. ISBN-13: 978-0-470-60825-8

HFR, HealthesearchFund.org. 55 Surprising Divorce Statistics of Second Marriages. http://healthresearchfunding.org/55-surprising-divorce-statistics-second-marriages/

Johnson, R. (2012). *That's My Girl: How a Father's Love Protects and Empowers His Daughter*. Rewell, Baker Publishing Group: Grand Rapids, MI, USA. ISBN-13: 978-0-8007-3383-4

Kefler, R. (2001). *You Are Who You Are For A Reason*. A Poem by Russell Kefler. Discipleship Tape Ministries Inc., Into His Likeness Radio: San Antonio, TX, USA. Retrieved October 16, 2016, at http://www.dtm.org/life-lessons/read/selected-poems-by-russell-(readprint)

Kiyosaki, R. T. (1997). *Rich Dad, Poor Dad: What the Rich Teach Their Kids About Money*. Warner Books, Cashflow Technologies Inc.: New York, NY, USA. ISBN-10: 0-446-67745-0

Leaf, C. (2013). *Switch On Your Brain: The Key to Peak Happiness, Thinking, and Health*. Baker Books, Baker Publishing Group: Grand Rapids, MI, USA. ISBN-13: 978-1-4412-4464-2

Marsh, C. (2000). *Dare to Dream: Inspirational Insights for Achieving a Successful and Fulfilling Life*. True Colors, Incorporated Publishing: Nashville, TN, USA. ISBN-13: 978-1893320215

Maunder, L., & Cameron, L. (2013*). Abuse: Information for Adults Physically, Emotionally, or Sexually Abused as Children,* Second Edition. Patient Information Centre: Northumberland, Tyne and Wear NHS Foundation Trust. ISBN-13: 978-1909664166

Moulton Marston, W. (2016). *DISC Theory and DISC Personality Traits*. Retrieved October 16, 2016, at www.discinsights.com

The Myers-Briggs Foundation (2016). *Myers-Briggs Type Indicator*. Retrieved October 16, 2016, at http://www.myersbriggs.org

True Colors International (2016). *True Colors Personality Test*. Retrieved October 16, 2016, at https://truecolorsintl.com/

Van Harmelen, A. L., Van Tol, M. J., Van Der Wee, N. J. A., Veltman, D. J., Aleman, A., Spinhoven, P., Van Buchem, M. A., Zitman, F. G., Penninx, B. W. J. H., & Elzinga, B. M. (2010). Reduced medial prefrontal cortex volume in adults reporting childhood emotional maltreatment. BIOLOGICAL PSYCHIATRY, 68:9, PP. 832-838.

Warren, R. (2007). *The Purpose Driven Life: What on Earth Am I Here for?* Expanded Edition. Zondervan, HarperCollins: Grand Rapids, MI, USA. ISBN-13: 978-0310337508

Watson, M. (2014). *Dad, I Really Need You: A Guide for Connecting with Your Daughter's Heart*. Harvest House Publishers: Eugene, OR, USA. ISBN-13: 978-7369-5840-0

Wikipedia (2016). *Four Temperaments: The Four Temperaments of Hippocratic Humor Theory*. Retrieved October 16, 2016, at https://en.wikipedia.org/wiki/Four_temperaments

Pictures: Inspirestock International c 123RF

Copyright: <a
href='https://www.123rf.com/profile_stockbroker'>stockbroker / 123RF
Stock Photo</a> Image ID: 42109253, Copyright: Cathy
Yeulet (Follow)Copyright: <a
href='https://www.123rf.com/profile_olgalebedeva'>olgalebedeva / 123RF
Stock Photo</a> Image ID : 31848485, Copyright : Olga Lebedeva (Follow)
Copyright: <a href='https://www.123rf.com/profile_racorn'>racorn /
123RF Stock Photo</a> Image ID : 21109995, Copyright : racorn (Follow)
Copyright: <a href='https://www.123rf.com/profile_reamonn'>reamonn /
123RF Stock Photo</a> Image ID : 12235332, Copyright : Anton
Maltsev (Follow)
Copyright: <a
href='https://www.123rf.com/profile_inspirestock'>inspirestock / 123RF
Stock Photo</a> Image ID : 44040198, Copyright : Josep Suria (Follow)
Copyright: <a
href='https://www.123rf.com/profile_inspirestock'>inspirestock / 123RF
Stock Photo</a> Image ID : 26272061, Copyright : Inspirestock
International - Exclusive Contributor (Follow)
Copyright: <a
href='https://www.123rf.com/profile_inspirestock'>inspirestock / 123RF
Stock Photo</a> Image ID : 13714186, Copyright : Dmitriy
Melnikov (Follow)
Copyright: <a
href='https://www.123rf.com/profile_inspirestock'>inspirestock / 123RF
Stock Photo</a> Image ID : 10197901, Copyright : Wavebreak Media
Ltd (Follow)
Copyright: <a href='https://www.123rf.com/profile_rocketclips'>rocketclips
/ 123RF Stock Photo</a> Image ID : 33804140, Copyright : Mark
Adams (Follow)
Copyright: <a
href='https://www.123rf.com/profile_inspirestock'>inspirestock / 123RF
Stock Photo</a> Image ID : 26267866, Copyright : Inspirestock
International - Exclusive Contributor (Follow)
Copyright: <a href='https://www.123rf.com/profile_dpullman'>dpullman /
123RF Stock Photo</a> Image ID : 14453438, Copyright : Darren
Pullman (Follow)
Copyright: <a href='https://www.123rf.com/profile_in8finity'>in8finity /
123RF Stock Photo</a> Image ID : 63118116, Copyright : Sergey
Siz`kov (Follow)
Copyright: <a href='https://www.123rf.com/profile_refluo'>refluo / 123RF
Stock Photo</a> Image ID : 31452149, Copyright : Anna
Bogatyreva (Follow)